Praise for
EXPONENTIAL
and Jeff Rosenblum

"Jeff's *Exponential* is a must-read for disruptive marketers who want to make an impact and break barriers. Jeff shares invaluable lessons for his readers about the importance of establishing a strong brand and why the safe business decision isn't always the right one."

—Brian Halligan, cofounder and CEO of HubSpot

"This book is an absolute home run! Through laugh-out-loud personal anecdotes and a rich history with some of the world's largest brands, Mr. Rosenblum delivers one fascinating insight after another. Anyone with a growth mindset should read this book."

—Joe Mason, CMO of Allianz Partners

"Everything has changed. Brands need to adapt. This book will make you laugh and cry—and gives you an action plan to modernize your marketing."

—Catherine Captain, CMO, GE Digital

"Jeff has a keen understanding of the power of brands and the role they play in our everyday lives. *Exponential* provides an insightful look at how brands are built by empowering the end-user to come along on the journey. It's a fast-paced read from an avid storyteller who has never been afraid to take the road less traveled."

—Lisa Checchio, EVP and CMO at
Wyndham Hotels & Resorts

"It's astounding to me how many brands cling to obsolete methodologies, practices, and habits. In his irreverent, take-no-prisoners style, Jeff Rosenblum takes us on a journey designed to incinerate conventional business thinking. Just like he did in his prior book, *Friction*, he forced me to look inward at my own marketing beliefs and step away from my safe place. I can't thank him enough."

> —**Kerry Graeber,** VP, Division Manager,
> Motorcycle/ATV Sales & Marketing,
> Suzuki Motor USA

"With compelling insight and clarity, *Exponential* delivers the road map for how to avoid the safe path that leads to irrelevance, and instead fully embrace the risks that enable companies to build an authentic place in consumers' lives. Jeff Rosenblum's incisive truth-telling is required reading for forward-leaning companies that have the courage to earn their customers' attention and loyalty through radical transparency and empowerment."

> —**Mark Jamison,** Global Head of Product
> Innovation & Design, Visa Inc.

"Every customer interaction is an opportunity to grow or diminish brand equity. In *Exponential*, Jeff does what he does best in laying out a practical, personal, and holistic approach to modern brand building and the organizational alchemy necessary to pull it off."

> —**Chris Crayner,** Chief Digital Officer of
> NBCUniversal Parks & Resorts

"Jeff Rosenblum is a pioneer in the industry. This book presents a bold new look at how brands should redefine their relationships with customers by empowering them."

> —**George Newman,** Associate Professor of
> Management and Marketing at Yale

"With an authentic and raw voice, Jeff hits at the challenges and paths to success in front of advertisers and brand builders in our new reality. Everyone will take away important truths about connecting with consumers and building a sustainable brand."
—**Jordan Dewitt,** Vice President, Creative,
Capital One

"I can't think of a single time that I didn't leave a conversation with Jeff Rosenblum mentally exploding with ideas and follow-ups from his way of seeing the world. He is totally unique, one of the most creative minds I know and I learn from him every time we interact. This book is all of Jeff and then some."
—**Trevor Price,** founder and CEO of Oxeon
Holdings, founder and General Partner,
Town Hall Ventures

"In the engaging style that defines him, Jeff Rosenblum lays out some timeless truths about the marketing discipline . . . that analytic rigor and creative insight are key ingredients but brands that outperform first and foremost remain true and authentic to their reason for being."
—**Jarvis Bowers,** VP of Marketing at Pearson

"Exponential should be required reading for every marketing leader. The old ways of advertising are out. Jeff gives us a well-written and much-needed road map to harness the purpose of brands, truly connect with consumers, and drive exponential growth for companies."
—**Steve Hartman,** Investor, Advisor, and former
Chief Marketing Officer of Eddie Bauer

"In a masterclass in marketing, and a warning to businesses unwilling to change, Jeff Rosenblum makes an evidence-based case for a clear brand purpose grounded in consumer empowerment. What a great read and lesson!"
> —**Brand Barrett,** Director, Brand Agency Relations at Capital One

"Jeff is not only a great writer with wisdom to share, but he is very handsome. I know that doesn't translate well to a written medium, but if you picture him as you read, it enhances the experience."
> —**Joel Stein,** author of *Man Made* and *In Defense of Elitism*

"I've been working with this maniac for over two decades and have loved *almost* every minute of it. This book captures the lessons we've learned the hard way and provides some great actionable advice."
> —**Jordan Berg,** Founding Partner of Questus

"I thought my son was a complete knucklehead who couldn't construct a sentence, but this book is legitimately good. He said if I write a recommendation, he'll buy me lunch. So, get this book."
> —**Neil Rosenblum,** author's father and market research teacher

EXP**O**NENTIAL

EXPONENTIAL

Transform Your Brand by Empowering Instead of Interrupting

JEFF ROSENBLUM

Mc
Graw
Hill

New York   Chicago   San Francisco   Athens   London   Madrid
Mexico City   Milan   New Delhi   Singapore   Sydney   Toronto

2 3 4 5 6 7 8 9   LCR   26 25 24 23 22 21

ISBN   978-1-264-26814-6
MHID   1-264-26814-9

e-ISBN   978-1-264-26815-3
e-MHID   1-264-26815-7

Library of Congress Cataloging-in-Publication Data

Names: Rosenblum, Jeff, author.
Title: Exponential : transform your brand by empowering instead of
    interrupting / Jeff Rosenblum.
Description: New York, NY : McGraw Hill, 2022. | Includes bibliographical
    references and index.
Identifiers: LCCN 2021034863 (print) | LCCN 2021034864 (ebook) |
    ISBN 9781264268146 (hardback) | ISBN 9781264268153 (ebook)
Subjects: LCSH: Branding (Marketing) | Advertising--Brand name
    products.
Classification: LCC HF5415.1255 .R677 2021 (print) | LCC HF5415.1255
    (ebook) | DDC 658.8/27--dc23
LC record available at https://lccn.loc.gov/2021034863
LC ebook record available at https://lccn.loc.gov/2021034864

McGraw Hill books are available at special quantity discounts to use as premiums and sales promotions or for use in corporate training programs. To contact a representative, please visit the Contact Us pages at www.mhprofessional.com.

Dedicated to Jena, Kayla, Tyler, and Kelly.
After all of this writing, I still can't find the right
words to express how much I love you.

CONTENTS

Brands stand naked in front of their customers. They are now defined by their behavior, not their messaging.

1 Introduction to the Advertising Revolution

The most vivid memory of my childhood is when I was eight years old and pointing a knife at my 11-year-old brother. It was a carving knife, 12 inches long and razor sharp, with two points at the tip for picking up large hunks of meat.

My brother was a foot away in our kitchen, pointing an 8-inch chef's knife at me. We were both in perfect form, standing sideways, bouncing on our toes, ready to strike. We both have our superhero pajamas on and we were laughing that uncontrollably wild, beautiful, insane laughter kids get when they're up past their bedtime and hyperactivity has taken over. Our parents were out of the house. Our babysitter was scared shitless.

The top drawer was where we kept the knives. After I took the serrated knife out and pointed it at my brother with the laugh of a madman, he grabbed the chef's knife.

We circled clockwise. I jabbed at him first. He sidestepped my jab and replied with a slash that barely missed my torso. The insane laughter grew.

We were best friends and had no intention of hurting each other. But our babysitter, watching us circle each other in front of the toaster oven, didn't know that. I don't remember his name. He was a nice guy, a teenager with dark curly hair. He didn't smell weird like our other babysitter.

"No!" the babysitter screamed.

"Yes!" I yelled between gasps of laughter.

"No!" he screamed again, with increasing desperation.

"Yes!" I replied, laughing even harder.

He should have grabbed my arm, but instead he lunged for the knife handle. I pulled the knife back just as he grabbed it. Twelve inches of serrated edge, designed to cut the thickest of steaks, tore through the skin and flesh of his thumb, down to the bone.

There was blood everywhere. My brother called 911, and we went through rolls upon rolls of paper towels, soaking them red, until an ambulance arrived. After that, we never saw him again.

I remember where and how we stood, the design of our pajamas, the sound of our laughter, the red blood pouring out of that poor guy's hand, down his arm, and dripping from his elbow into a pool on the kitchen floor.

But there's one thing I absolutely do not recall: the punishment. Because I didn't get in trouble at all. Not one lick. My parents didn't even yell at me. It was as if the incident hadn't even happened.

Years later, I learned that my father hated violence, aggression, and confrontations because he was rebelling against his own father, a literal gangster. My grandfather was affiliated with Murder Inc., the Jewish mafia born out of Prohibition that committed an estimated 1,000 murders across New York.

The stories I heard as a kid were fantastic. His brother, my great uncle, once got hit in the head with an ax. Somehow he survived, but it left a horizontal divot across his forehead. During holiday family gatherings, he entertained the kids by putting the butt end of lit cigarettes in his forehead. When their other brother went to prison, the family armed themselves with shotguns and busted him out.

My favorite among all those stories is my teenage father going out on the town with my grandfather. Because he was a big shot in the liquor business, my grandfather had a reserved table at the front of the Copacabana, where he took my father to see Sammy Davis Jr. and other legendary performers. It was like that scene in *Goodfellas* when Henry Hill and his date bypass the line, go through the kitchen of the Copa, and have a table waiting for them in front of the stage. The only difference is that my father and grandfather didn't go through the side door. They marched right through the front door like Jewish gangster royalty.

Unfortunately for my father, that's about the only positive story of his childhood. The truth is that my grandfather was a monster who punched, kicked, and threw my father around. Absolutely horrible abuse. My father was beaten so badly that at one point, he hit the ceiling while getting thrown across the room. He said time seemed to move in slow motion as he realized it was going to be a big drop to the floor.

While this type of violence is often passed down to the next generation, my father decided to go in the complete opposite direction. He was honest and friendly, and never even raised his voice to his kids, let alone his fists. I admire him for choosing that path, but it had the unintended effect of teaching me that I could get away with anything. If there was no punishment for cutting off my babysitter's thumb, there were truly no limits.

A childhood without punishments turned me into a chronic risk taker. Not the long-haired, skydiving, rock-climbing kind of risk taker. Admittedly, I've crashed a motorcycle, been knocked out in a kickboxing match, and flown across Africa in the aeronautical equivalent of a 1968 Dodge Dart. But most of my risks have been business-related. My comfort around risk is the greatest gift my parents ever gave me.

Despite barely graduating college, I begged my way into a job working for a team of Harvard MBAs who were doing research for the world's most influential brands. When the internet hit, I took a risk by convincing the founders to throw out their business model and became one of a handful of people pioneering the field of internet research. Despite the fact that I was still a zit-faced kid, I was soon helping these brands drive data-driven strategies.

Then, I realized something else: The data we acquired proved that most advertising didn't work. So, I quit my job at 27 and started an agency with my best friend, even though neither of us had even stepped foot in one before. In making each of these major, life-changing decisions, I always focused on the potential upside instead of worrying about the potential downside.

This high tolerance for risk is essential in business today. We are in the midst of one of the greatest revolutions in history. Time after time, however, I see brands choose the safe path, ignoring new opportunities and continuing to do what they've always done. But safe fails every time. Safe advertising is invisible. Safe business models get disrupted. Safe executives get replaced.

Early Lessons in Advertising Psychology

My interest in research and advertising started soon after the incident with my babysitter. As an act of rebellion against his gangster father, my father became a complete square.

Despite being invited to play minor league ball for the Brooklyn Dodgers, he took the first job offered to him and spent his evenings reading about science and psychology. Every night at the dinner table he would discuss whatever experiments he had been reading about. He especially enjoyed conducting his own experiments to prove how gullible consumers are and used us as his guinea pigs.

For example, one night he poured soda into different paper cups and asked us to taste each one and rank our preferences. This was a variation on the famous Pepsi Challenge. We had Coke, Pepsi, RC Cola, and a generic brand. We soon realized that there was little distinguishable difference between them. The only reason we each had a favorite cola was the packaging and the marketing. We did dozens of experiments like that, where we'd rate different products, only for my father to reveal that quality and price had almost no relationship to each other.

His own father, the ex-bootlegger, had proved this fact to him decades earlier. He frequently invited his friends from the liquor business to his apartment in Brooklyn and used my dad as a bartender. My father's first task before the guests arrived was to fill empty bottles of the most expensive liquor with the cheapest, crappiest booze available. My father watched as these industry insiders pompously patted each other on the back, raised their drinks above their heads, and ceremoniously toasted each other with the phrase "nectar of the gods!" They didn't realize that they were basically drinking piss out of fancy bottles.

Recognizing that even industry insiders couldn't tell the difference, my grandfather, who ran a distillery called Ron Zorro, raised prices and increased sales by changing the stickers on his bottles from "Aged Two Years" to "Aged Four Years" and eventually to 8, 10, and 12. The booze inside had actually only been aged for a few weeks.

My father was disgusted by how easily people could be manipulated by false promises, fancy logos, and dishonest packaging. He set up the experiments at the dinner table because he didn't want his kids to be fooled by advertising. But his noble intentions backfired. Instead of being repulsed by the power of brands and advertising, I was fascinated by it. I wanted in on that action. I started paying more attention to commercials than I ever did to my schoolwork.

The Misunderstood Revolution

The cozy, often dishonest relationships between brands and consumers have gone through massive change. At the core of the advertising revolution is how brands communicate with consumers. Traditionally, that has been a one-way street that was only occasionally disrupted. But search, social, and mobile technology have fundamentally changed the ways that people interact with businesses. Consumers today avoid traditional advertising. They have ratings, reviews, and expert guidance at their fingertips. They know the truth, and they know it in real time. This changes not just how businesses should communicate, but how they should live, think, behave, and operate.

Most businesses made the mistake of assuming that digital was a simple replacement for analog—that the difference was a delivery system, not a fundamental change in dynamics. Instead of seeing an opportunity to invent new forms of advertising, most brands just adapted these shiny new tools to their stodgy old strategy of interruptive marketing. Thirty-second TV spots became thirty-second pre-rolls. Print ads became banner ads. Junk mail became spam. Radio spots became podcast spots.

Soon after, brands shifted their focus to social media and offered us cat memes and ice bucket challenges, not realizing that the underpinnings of advertising had completely changed. Creativity isn't the solution. It's simply an ingredient.

Today, brands stand naked in front of their customers. They are now defined by their behavior, not their messaging. This isn't simply an advertising challenge. It's a strategic challenge. It's a data challenge. It's a culture challenge. It's a leadership challenge.

Empowerment Leads to Exponential Growth

The story about my babysitter's bloody thumb was a bait and switch. I baited you in with a story, but I want to switch to some heady topics in this book, including statistics and neuroscience. Core to the story is the concept of exponential growth. Exponential isn't simply an adjective. It's a mathematical function based on compounded growth. For example, if a key metric compounds 10 percent annually, the original amount and the 10 percent each grow by 10 percent every year. As they compound, they grow dramatically, creating a pattern that looks like the right side of a *U*. It starts relatively horizontal, but when compounding kicks in, the graph rapidly becomes more vertical.

Here's an example that financial investors use to demonstrate the power of compounding: If you were offered a choice between an immediate cash payment of $1 million or a magic penny that doubled every day for 30 days, which one would you take? Most people would take the immediate million dollars. But if you double one penny for 30 days, the final amount is over $5 million!

Unlike linear growth, which can start strong and remains constant, exponential growth often starts much slower. Eventually, however, key inputs take hold and the line bends dramatically upward. Venture capitalists refer to exponential growth as the "hockey stick." If you look at the stock charts of the world's top technology brands—Facebook, Netflix, Google, Apple, and so on—they all have this coveted shape.

Brand evangelists who actively proselytize for brands with word-of-mouth marketing are critical to exponential growth because the conversations compound as each person shares positive feedback about a brand with multiple people.

Creating exponential curves isn't all about being creative. It's scientific. There's a methodical process that works to build billion-dollar brands. Rather than focus on superficial and interruptive messages, brands can focus on a chronological sequence rooted in the indisputable fact that the audience is now in control.

Brands must first nail their purpose—the role that they are going to play in people's lives. Then they need to develop their internal culture—the everyday behaviors that bring a brand's purpose to life. With that foundation in place, brands can then invest in empowering content and meaningful experiences. Of course, advertising still has a massively important role, so long as brands focus first on purpose, behavior, and culture before they focus on external messaging.

Brands that achieve exponential growth these days know that incrementalism is the enemy. Improving advertising metrics by managing two to three arcane variables pales in performance when compared to empowering people throughout the entire consumer journey. For some in the advertising industry, this is anathema. For others, it's the nirvana. Regardless, the team required for the modern environment is not the team that was effective for the past century.

People Want More from Brands Than Interruptions and Superficial Messages

Brands can no longer succeed through targeted advertising and clever messaging. In an age of total transparency, success or failure is driven by behavior, not advertising. Some brands are dominating the competition, while others—including many household names—are going broke. The fundamental difference between those two groups is to what extent they empower their customers.

Advertising is shifting from technology-fueled messages that interrupt the consumer journey to data-connected content that carries people through the consumer journey. It's about removing friction, understanding emotional and functional needs at every step along the way, and moving people toward their goals. The brands that use this approach to improve the lives of their customers build an army of evangelists who carry their brand messages forward more effectively than traditional advertising.

This new type of advertising doesn't need to be a Patagonia-inspired public service initiative promising to save the world. While those efforts are great, most people don't wake up in the morning expecting brands to hug the trees and save the manatees. They simply want their own lives improved, one small step at a time.

Empowerment can be focused on educating people, like Fender's efforts to help people play better guitar through their Fender Play platform, or MasterClass's efforts to teach people about their favorite topics through online videos, or Google's efforts to enable people to leverage data via their Google Think platform.

Empowerment can be about inspiring people with content like 805 Beer's video series about people enjoying outdoor adventures. It can be something philanthropic like Bombas providing socks to the homeless. It can be about making shopping more fun and easy like Restoration Hardware turning stores into immersive experiences or Warby Parker making glasses easier and more affordable to buy. Perhaps, empowerment is simply baked right into a product like The Farmer's Dog supporting both farms and families by delivering fresh food for man's best friend.

Advertising is not dead. That false eulogy has been written before. It just needs to be redefined to be about immersive content and experiences, not just interruptive messages. If we look at the automobile industry to highlight the issue, we see that the average car buyer spends a total of 13 hours doing research over the course of six months. An aggressive effort by a manufacturer to reach each customer through traditional interruptive advertising would be about twelve 30-second exposures, in some mix of TV commercials, social media videos, radio spots, billboards, or other media. I think we can all agree that seeing the same ad 12 times would be annoying, even if it came in slightly different formats.

The bigger point is that even if those traditional ads are engaging and meaningful rather than annoying, the 12 exposures equal only six minutes of engagement, which leaves another 12 hours and 54 minutes that the customer is doing research without the manufacturer's participation. If the brand gets super aggressive and doubles its budget, they'll hit each person with 12 minutes of content, leaving 12 hours and 48 minutes for independent research.

Interruptive advertising might be enough to get people *into* the sales funnel but not *through* the sales funnel. That's why empowering content is so critical.

The common thread between all of these exponential brands is that they have found an authentic and valuable place in their customers' lives. When brands create content that makes people's lives better, they can stop worrying about whether enough people are watching their 30-second ads. They can get fans to invest 30 minutes, or even 30 hours, by engaging them with immersive content that they actually want to watch and read.

Exponential brands also have rethought the totality of their behavior—because in a naked world, they are completely exposed. Embracing transparency isn't as simple as doing away with bad behavior, and it's sure as hell not as simple as virtue signaling about the latest trendy topic. It's about a fundamental shift in corporate behavior. It's about first focusing inward to nail a brand's purpose and culture before focusing outward with content that improves people's lives.

Advertising Technology Has Shifted from Asynchronous to Synchronous

Over 50 years ago, NASA sent a man to the moon on Apollo 11. Now, every person with discretionary income is walking around with a supercomputer in their pocket that has 1 million times the memory and 100,000 times the processing power of the computer that was on that rocket. With that power comes unprecedented information. The average adult consumes five times more information every day than people did 50 years ago.

Yet, the revolution isn't simply about consumers gaining access to information. It's about a shift in information flow from asynchronous to synchronous. For the past century, communication was asynchronous—one way. Brands created stories and the audience listened.

Like the internet today, television was once a high-tech miracle. Commercials and other brand communication weren't considered annoying or frivolous in the 1950s; they were embraced because they brought comedians and TV stars into our homes. Audiences loved those early commercials and believed their messages. Where else could people learn about the latest packaged foods and appliances?

But before long, brands shattered that trust. Fred Flintstone and Barney Rubble went behind the house, made a few misogynistic jokes about their wives, lit up some Winstons, and had some laughs. Millions of people started to smoke. Millions died. Decades later, the tobacco CEOs were forced to testify in Congress about how they had lied in their commercials. Over time, trust between consumers and corporations became completely broken.

To combat this lack of trust, brands built stronger relationships with TV networks and developed a model based on repeating the same messages over and over until they bludgeoned the human brain into a willingness to buy.

Then, they ramped up the creativity. In a great example of a dead cat bounce, Budweiser launched the "Whassup" campaign, which became a pop culture phenomenon with millions of people parroting the twentysomething bros on their couches. The commercials won the coveted Grand Clio award and increased sales by a whopping 2.4 million barrels. Seeing this success, other brands pushed their creativity to unprecedented heights, but with rapidly diminishing returns. In the decade that followed the Whassup campaign, Budweiser spent a quarter of a billion dollars on Super Bowl ads alone. But quality eventually triumphed over marketing, and the King of Beers was dethroned with market share that plummeted in the new millennium.

Business communication is now synchronous, like any healthy relationship. Consumers tell brands what they want, either explicitly through text and speech or implicitly by their behavior. Exponential brands respond with optimized products, content, experiences, and even traditional advertisements.

I'm amazed at how many people in the advertising industry either still don't get that this is the path to success or don't know what to do about it. So they keep doing the same old things—variations on interruptive ads—with results that get worse and worse. It's institutional insanity, and it wastes a huge percentage of the $242 billion spent on American advertising every year.

Empowerment Drives Exponential Bottom-Line Results

There's proof that empowerment works in bottom-line financial results. One of the most remarkable studies comes from Raj Sisodia and a team of researchers who studied the results of Conscious Capitalism, a philosophy of doing business that incorporates the principles of brand purpose, stakeholder interdependence, servant leadership, and corporate culture. His data reveals that companies that adhere to these principles outperformed the market by 9 to 1 over a

10-year period. That's over 1,100 percent growth versus 123 percent for the S&P 500. Did you ever kick yourself because you didn't buy Google stock 10 years ago? That's the type of performance that Sisodia's team found.

Sisodia isn't unique in his interest in empowering brands. Some of the world's leading investors, tirelessly seeking out a competitive advantage, have also conducted extensive research on the topic. JUST, which was founded by a group of investors that includes billionaire Paul Tudor Jones, analyzed the Russell 1000, measuring share performance against a number of metrics that indicate empowerment. The resulting survey found that the top quintile of companies showed 14 percent higher annualized returns and 7 percent lower volatility compared with the bottom 20 percent. That's massive in the finance world.

Bank of America/Merrill Lynch also reported to clients on a similar finding—that a strategy of buying stocks of the best-behaved companies would have beaten the market by up to 3 percentage points a year over the previous five years. In an industry where you make millions in salary and bonuses by beating the benchmark by half a point, 3 points is a landslide.

One thing that hasn't changed is that the role of advertising is still to generate demand. The difference between good marketers and great marketers is that great marketers drive stronger return on investment. They don't just drive demand, they drive profitable demand. But no amount of traditional advertising can outperform the competition 9 to 1.

Those kinds of exponential results can only come from embracing empowerment at every level of a company.

Perhaps the most exciting part of this finding is that when corporations shift their focus to empowerment, they can make a real difference in the world. Of the 100 largest economic entities in the world, 69 of them are corporations. This proportion has doubled in the past decade and shows no signs of slowing down. The world's top 10 corporations generate more revenue in total than 180 of the poorest countries combined. Walmart, Apple, and Shell are richer than Russia, Belgium, and Sweden. Changes in corporate behavior can impact the lives of billions of people around the world.

Corporations will naturally gravitate toward whatever produces profit. That's not a bad thing. It's simply the way the game is played. Football is about touchdowns. Basketball is about buckets. Business is about profits. Trying to add a divergent metric into the equation will fail every time. Adding a metric that works only in the short term won't lead to sustained focus. But empowerment leads to profits, and that's a sustainable strategic underpinning that will continue in perpetuity, regardless of the latest technological advancements or marketing fads.

Some of the world's most influential and creative people work in marketing. They are excited about the shift to a model based on empowerment. They see that there's an opportunity to conduct business in a way that benefits both behemoth corporations and folks living on Main Street. They are ready to lead the revolution.

I Got Bloodied So You Don't Have To

It's fair to say that, in a lot of ways, it hasn't been helpful for my career to keep telling people that the conventional wisdom is wrong. As Michael Lewis wrote in *Moneyball* about the statistical revolution in baseball, "The first guy through the wall . . . he always gets bloody . . . always."

After we launched our agency, it would have been a lot easier for us to create the same types of superficial, non-empowering advertising that brands have produced for decades. There've been times when we've been bloodied by trying to give our clients exponential results driven through empowerment rather than the incremental results that come from doing things the traditional way.

It's also important to note that my comfort with risk has caused me to crash and burn a few times, and throughout this book we will learn from those mistakes. I'm not scared to admit I've been brought to tears by poor decision-making. Hopefully, this book helps others avoid my blunders.

We began with a gory story about how I nearly severed a kid's thumb. From here on, I promise that the blood spilled will be more metaphorical than literal. But the disruptions to the status quo will be no less dramatic.

Three Exponential Takeaways

- Advertising is shifting from technology-fueled messages that interrupt the consumer journey to data-connected content that carries people through the consumer journey.

- Brands that improve the lives of their customers build an army of evangelists who carry their brand messages forward more effectively than any form of traditional advertising.

- When brands create content that makes people's lives better, they can stop worrying about whether enough people are watching their 30-second ads. They can get fans to invest 30 hours by engaging them with content that they actually want.

And One Question to Ponder

If most traditional ads are so damn annoying, why do brands continue to collectively invest billions in them?

Successful modern advertising is simply a value exchange. Consumers give their hard-earned dollars, data, and evangelism in exchange for content that informs and inspires.

2 Modern Advertising Is a Value Exchange

We started our agency with two desks, one chair, a dying laptop, and the last pack of Marlboros we would ever enjoy. We had one simple idea: marry data and creativity to redefine advertising into something that brought meaning and value to people's lives. Other than that, we were clueless.

While taking turns sharing our only chair, we set out on our first gig creating a platform of millions of consumers who would be available for internet research. The project would pay our bills for three months, at which point we would run out of money and prove to our friends and family that we were in over our heads.

On our very first day, I installed Photoshop on my laptop and got to work on the consumer interface for the project. When my draft looked pretty good to me, I called my new business partner, Jordan, over to check out the design, plus a couple of rough ads to promote the site. He took one look at it and said, "Take Photoshop off your computer right now and never reinstall it, or we are closing this agency." That was the end of my career in the creative department.

So, I hit my Rolodex to try to find new clients. The concept of revolutionizing advertising seemed glaringly obvious. The big challenge was getting a major brand to take a chance on us. It's one thing to have a good idea; it's another to have a track record. We hit our networks to set up meetings, then launched an idea to overcome the friction. On a corner of the whiteboard in our makeshift conference room, I scribbled sloppily:

Nike 6/22
Microsoft 7/1
Apple 7/7

We weren't working with Nike, Microsoft, or Apple at that point, nor did we have meetings scheduled with them. We didn't even know anyone at those companies. But every time we met with potential clients, Jordan and I sat them across from the whiteboard, and watched their eyes drift away from ours and to the corner with my scribbles.

I had a strong track record in research, but we needed recognizable brand names to make potential clients feel safe hiring us for advertising. We knew that decision makers at brands are only human and were inundated with information, distractions, and pitches from agencies. Few people have the time or expertise to fully assess a business. They look for shortcuts: the sound of a car door when it closes, the price of a new watch, the smile on a salesperson's face, the packaging for a new tech product, the cleanliness of a restaurant bathroom. The big brand names on our whiteboard helped us create shortcuts for prospective clients.

I've learned over time that this approach is rooted in social affirmation. It's a critical marketing ingredient that explains why recommendations from friends and family are the single most trusted information source for purchase decisions. Brands now obsess about how to generate social affirmation.

At the time, I wasn't thinking about deep psychological principles. I was simply looking for a client brave enough to try our new theories for building brands by blending data and creativity. Our whiteboard might have been stretching the truth, but it worked. Before long we had enough clients to buy out an initial investor, hire four new team members and move to a bigger office.

Stumbling into the Dot-Com Boom

Let's back up for a moment to explain how I got to this point in my career. It was dumb luck that I landed in San Francisco at the start of the dot-com boom. I went to college in Vermont, an idyllic place where I met my future wife, my future business partner, and some lifelong friends. I was a good test taker and presenter so my grades were pretty good, but I was physiologically incapable of sitting through classes. Since I was raised without any repercussions for bad behavior, I decided to simply not go.

I couldn't wait to start marketing in the real world, so I started a business by selling custom T-shirts and hats door to door. The University of Vermont was filled with hippies, but I decided to make a T-shirt with a red circle and slash through the Grateful Dead Steal Your Face icon, with the text "I'll be Grateful When They're Dead." Most students threw me out of their dorm rooms with disdain, but the minority who weren't Deadheads appreciated my audacity. They bought my merch as a small way to rebel against the hippie majority. I then upsold them on higher-margin hats and watched them pick up their dorm phones and call friends to see if they wanted me to come over. These were early lessons in niche marketing and the power of evangelism.

When I graduated, I didn't exactly have a line of industry-leading clients beating down my door for an interview, so I took a year off to live with friends in Lake Tahoe. We always had money for partying, but we didn't have money for basic necessities. We had one working light bulb in the whole house. You had to lick your fingers to unscrew the hot bulb and walk it from room to room to see. We didn't pay for heat during one of the most epic winters in Tahoe history. We were surrounded by eight feet of snow, and the temperature was subfreezing in the house. One of our Ivy League graduate friends came from New York City to visit us for a ski trip. He lasted a day.

But Tahoe was the crazy luck that I needed. It put me on the doorstep of Silicon Valley. When it was time to get a real job, I went to the nearest city, San Francisco, the epicenter of tech world. After weeks of cold-calling companies that I found in the yellow pages, I finally came across King, Brown & Partners, an agency that specialized in marketing research and strategy. It was run by two great guys, Haldane King and Jacob Brown, who would soon teach me almost everything I know today about data, strategy, leadership, and culture. They had an impressive client list that included Disney, Intel, Discovery, Microsoft, American Express, Hewlett-Packard, and Bank of America.

After my interview, they called to turn me down. "We're a small shop. We've got all the resources we need. We don't have you in the budget. Thanks anyway." I was bummed, but after cooking at a restaurant in North Beach until 2 a.m. every night, I wrote them a letter and taped it to their door at 6 a.m. every morning for two weeks. If they were unimpressed with my résumé, I'd just have to inspire them with persistence. It was a war of attrition. Sure enough, after a few weeks, they were sick of my letters. Hal called to offer me a three-month internship. "That's the best we can do. At the end of three months, we'll figure out if it's working." Deal.

Pioneering the Field of Internet Research

One day, the partners at KB&P handed me a couple of floppy disks with some strange names printed on the labels: America Online and CompuServe. They asked me to connect the firm to the internet. I barely had sufficient attention span to install the software. Fast-forward a few days, and I was hooked. The more I played around with the internet, the more convinced I was that market research was about to go through a complete and total revolution.

As a project manager for KB&P, my mission was to collect accurate, affordable customer data using whatever tools were available. We would make telephone calls, send letters, meet people at the mall, and set up traditional focus groups. The challenge was that data was expensive. Every person we spoke to cost money. Every question we asked cost money. My job was to figure out the optimal balance between sample size, data breadth, quality control, and total cost. It was impossible to optimize all of them concurrently.

At the time, I had a motorcycle. Not because it was cool. I bought it because it was cheap. At 500 cc's, it was woefully undersized to handle the winds and hills of San Francisco. My helmet was about three sizes too large and wobbled from side to side, bouncing off my cheeks. The padding inside was old and crumbling. It came free with the motorcycle and would be absolutely useless in a crash. Riding on the cycle, without the distractions of computers and meetings, was a powerful tool for clearing my head and coming up with new ideas for work.

After a week or so with the internet, I took a long ride outside of the city. Sure enough, I had a moment of clarity: I saw that the internet would soon become the ideal way to collect consumer data in a way that was broad, deep, and affordable. I walked into Jacob's office and explained that traditional research would become obsolete in the near future. Instead, we could use the internet to collect not only more data and faster data, but also better data. Jacob got it and gave me the nod to try it on a project.

At the time, there were only a handful of people in academia and a few others exploring the idea of using internet data for corporate clients. We were all young, ignorant, and excited about the fact that our entire industry was about to be upended. Projects that had previously taken six months could now be completed in six weeks. Soon, it would shift to six days.

I was still a kid, but I soon was leading strategic assignments for world-class clients. Companies like Microsoft, Disney, Netscape, Sun Microsystems, Discovery Channel, Intel, and Levi Strauss were relying on me to conduct strategic research. I often stayed at the office into the wee hours of the morning, fueled by caffeine and adrenaline while sifting through mountains of data.

It was the most dynamic moment in the history of business, and I was lucky enough to be at the epicenter, collecting data and building an innate understanding of exactly what people wanted from brands. I studied hundreds of thousands of data points from quantitative surveys. I spoke with hundreds of consumers in qualitative interviews. I performed usability tests with consumers using the latest websites and devices. I went shopping in malls and department stores with every demographic imaginable. I went into people's homes, closets, and living rooms to understand how people shop and live.

The most pronounced pattern in all of the data was that successful marketing initiatives created value for end users. The failed ones created friction. It was a simple dichotomy.

Uncovering the Difference between Transactional and Emotional Brands

I became obsessed with how emotions affected consumer behavior. I saw how brands could become part of people's core identities. I listened as they yelled about websites that they hated and cheered for brands that they loved. I saw that they never complained that a brand had made something too simple or too inspirational. Not once. Not ever.

As time went on, it became clear that two types of brands were emerging: transactional and emotional. Transactional brands offer the right product at the right price at the right time. Their ad campaigns let consumers know what they can do and what their capabilities are. If a consumer needs their product and the price seems fair, they'll buy, but they won't become a loyal customer. It's just a short-term, rational transaction.

Emotional brands, on the other hand, create irrational relationships—in the most positive sense of the word. They generate irrational enthusiasm. They charge irrationally high prices. Their customers literally ignore the competition. Some become evangelists who promote the brand on their clothing, in online reviews, and during impassioned conversations around the dinner table.

The key to creating these seemingly irrational relationships is to act in ways that would appear irrational for traditional advertisers. Rather than focusing on stories to convince and cajole, emotional brands are built by creating value for every step of the customer journey. They give more than they need to. They turn mundane interactions into meaningful moments. These moments of surprise and delight turn customers into evangelists. The data we collected about the word-of-mouth benefits from these evangelists revealed one of the most critical rules of modern business: the more evangelists you have, the fewer ads you need to buy.

At KB&P, we could see it plainly in the data we were collecting. A core type of research we conducted for clients was called a Usage and Attitudes survey. It focused on understanding how people feel about a brand and which levers can be pulled to make customers more satisfied and loyal. I watched as most brands desperately tried to increase their satisfaction ratings. But our client Disney, on the other hand, didn't target satisfaction as its goal. It used "magical" as its key performance indicator. This isn't just a matter of semantics. Disney set a fundamentally higher bar than any other company we researched. The entire culture of Disney was focused on this metric. As a result, Disney didn't simply have transactional relationships with its customers; the brand created emotional relationships that helped it become one of the most successful companies in the world.

I could see the macro issues in the quantitative data that revealed the unparalleled levels of satisfaction that

Disney generated. Then, I would meet Disneyphiles in the qualitative research and watch them actively promote the brand like it was a best friend. Like most emotional brands, Disney leveraged traditional advertising to generate awareness for its products and services. Advertising remains core to its playbook. But it also focuses on every single aspect of the customer journey to create a magical experience, right down to how cast members point to give directions in the theme parks. I spent thousands of hours with data from Disney's evangelists at an impressionable moment in my career, and it cemented my feelings about how content and experiences can be used to build brands that grow exponentially.

The data proved that modern advertising is simply a value exchange. Everyday customers function just like large corporations, but on a more subconscious level. They invest their hard-earned dollars and want a positive return on investment. The key to success for emotional brands compared to transactional brands is that they provide positive ROI at every touchpoint where they interact with customers. They don't rely only on traditional advertising to create their entire brand story.

The Data behind Interruptive Advertising

I became obsessed with using data to tell stories to help my clients take action. I turned the walls of our office into boards that looked like a scene in a police TV show. My goal was to tie together disparate data points to create a cohesive narrative so that marketers could take action. The idea was to help major corporations take a fundamentally different approach to building brands.

However, this storytelling approach was being used for an alarming type of research that I was also conducting. I was working with major media properties to help them make traditional interruptive advertising look effective. It became my forte. I never had to fudge any of the data, but I got really good at figuring out how to ask questions to tell a story that made each media property look like it could help brands grow and sell products. I learned how to structure a positive story based on ambiguous data. I conducted complicated segmentation, pre-post, and other analyses to show that traditional interruptive advertising was highly effective.

Every day, I found myself caught between two worlds, each fueled by data. In one world, I was figuring out exactly what consumers really want from brands. In the other world, I was creating stories that made it look like people really wanted more advertisements.

While I was "proving" the effectiveness of these ads, I was really seeing that traditional interruptive advertising doesn't work for much other than building awareness. It didn't lead to exponential growth. Most people in the advertising world are familiar with the late 19th century department store owner John Wanamaker's quote, "Half the money I spend on advertising is wasted; the trouble is

I don't know which half." Thanks to our newfound ability to do consumer research on the internet, I assumed that we would finally be able to identify and eliminate that wasted 50 percent. It turns out I was wrong, and so was Wanamaker. My data showed that the waste was closer to 90 percent.

When we asked people why they bought products, they almost never mentioned traditional advertising. Their purchases were influenced by recommendations from friends and empowering content they encountered in the consumer journey. The data clearly showed that although advertising played an important role, brands had better ways to apply strategy and creative than using TV commercials to interrupt people.

It occurred to me that a new kind of ad agency, one not tied to the traditions of the industry, could do a lot with the powerful data that I was seeing and studying. It would require big risks, but the potential upside could be massive—it would be a new kind of agency that really worked. If it could solve the problem of ineffective advertising, it should have every brand in the world beating down its door.

Around this time, my best friend from college, Jordan Berg, was working in digital design. Jordan was different from the rest of us in college. For most of us, our greatest accomplishment would be to flip upside down on a keg and chug beer for 20 seconds without having it come out of our noses. Jordan had different ambitions. One day I looked over his shoulder while he was sketching something in a notebook. It was beautiful. It was amazing. It was perfect.

I was shocked because I didn't realize he was so gifted with design. Jordan was light-years outside of anything I even dreamed of personally being able to do.

After college, Jordan had his own solo art shows at galleries in New York City. Celebrities like Johnny Depp bought his paintings. But Jordan didn't want to spend his life hoping for a lucky break to propel him to the upper echelons of the art world. He wanted to use his talents for more commercial applications. So, he found a job at a design agency that was creating immersive multimedia content for the web, long before broadband became ubiquitous. The websites and content he designed for clients were visually dramatic—and at least a decade ahead of their time.

One day Jordan sent me a link to a new site he was working on. It looked like the surface of Mars and slowly rotated across the screen. He called to ask me what I thought of it.

"It's awesome. But what do you do with it?" I replied.

"You run your mouse over each of the craters and get info, like corporate background."

"That's super cool. But who wants to navigate a website like that?" I asked.

"OK, smart guy. Show me what you're working on," he said.

So, I showed him some of the PowerPoint decks I was working on for my clients.

"Jeff, that's the most boring shit I've ever seen."

He was correct. My research was boring and worse still, it often wasn't even being used. My research clients were in separate departments from the product developers and advertisers. This separation meant that most of our findings simply collected dust.

Jordan and I realized that if we combined his cutting-edge designs with my data-driven insights, we could close the gap between data and creativity. We could figure out what people really want, and then deliver it with meaningful work. One day over beers, we convinced ourselves that since most advertising demonstrably sucked, we could easily do it better.

"Dude, we should start an agency," I said.

"Have you ever been in an agency?" he asked.

"No. Have you?"

"Nope."

"Let's do it."

At the time, I was arguing with Jacob, because my salary was still anchored to my original job as an assistant. One day I said, "I'm getting screwed because I'm doing incredible work for you, but I'm not getting paid accordingly." Amazingly, he was patient with my outburst. We talked about it for a few more weeks, until one day he walked into my office and declared verbatim, "We're going to unscrew you." He was doubling my salary.

A second-rate Hollywood screenwriter couldn't have created more cliché timing for what happened next. My phone rang while I was still processing this great news. Jacob assumed it was a client calling, so he told me to answer it as he stood in the doorway.

Jordan's voice on the phone said, "I did it."

"Did what?" I replied.

"I did it!"

"Did what??"

"I quit my job. We're going to start an agency."

"Holy shit, Jordan. I thought we were just drinking beers and talking smack. Are you serious?"

"Yes. We're doing it."

Two weeks later, we had an agency.

Muscle Memory Creates Institutional Insanity

Even today, I'm amazed at how many people in my industry act as if folks are still sitting patiently through TV commercials, admiring the flashy banner ads on their laptops, or watching closely as a YouTube pre-roll delays the video they really want to see. This kind of institutional insanity in corporate America is based on faith in a reach-and-frequency model, which the advertising industry has spent decades perfecting. It's a numbers game where the score is kept by how many people you can reach and how frequently you can interrupt them with a brand message.

But who feels good about being interrupted? In virtually no walk of life are interruptions considered a powerful tool for building relationships. They're one of the least appealing forms of communication. They are rude. They are annoying. They shut down the audience's ability to listen. Relying on interruptions is, frankly, insane. And yet it's been at the core of corporate strategy for decades—and continues to be for most companies. The money involved can be truly staggering. Out of the roughly $250 billion spent annually on advertising in the United States, the overwhelming majority goes to reach-and-frequency efforts via TV ads, pre-rolls, mobile pop-ups, billboards, and all the other crap that gets in the way of consumers doing what they want.

To be clear, interruptive advertising still works, up to a point. Decent brands can still be built, and decent results can still be created through traditional advertising. But nobody wakes up in the morning wanting merely decent results. We are simply asking traditional advertising to do too much. It's an effective weapon in the arsenal, but brands need to redirect their efforts toward immersive content that informs and inspires.

Every new technological advancement—web browsers, social media, mobile applications—seems to bring with it a new excuse to create interruptions. Marketers keep making ads, and the audience keeps running away. It's institutionalized muscle memory. Marketers keep doing the same thing because that's what they know how to do. It's not that brands are insufficiently intelligent or apathetic; it's that the whole system is broken. The leaders of the advertising industry were trained to use a tool that worked for a century before it was completely disrupted.

Just looking at one industry highlights the problem. The financial services industry, for example, serves over 300 billion digital impressions per year in the United States alone. That means if every single person in our country is online, ranging from infant to octogenarian, they are each served over 1,000 digital ads from just one industry. The data proves that the approach gets some results, but I equate it to trying to kill a grizzly bear with a BB gun. There are certainly more efficient solutions, particularly for complex industries where customers go on a journey to figure out which products they want to buy and which brands they want to support.

Soon after starting our agency, we started to work with one of the world's largest financial service companies. Its leaders wanted to prove that digital advertising works so that they could shift their investments from direct mail to digital. They owned an insurance product that was using digital advertising but was generating disappointing results. It provided a perfect opportunity to mathematically prove our theories. We helped them optimize their advertising creative and their media placements, and we generated a few percentage points of improvement. At a massive company, these incremental improvements equate to millions of dollars, and the client was happy.

But the powerful finding came when we examined the consumer journey and optimized the website where prospective customers were being sent. With a few modifications to the content and information flow, we were able to increase conversions 100 percent. Doubling conversions is not simply powerful because it generates more customers for every dollar spent, it also opens the floodgates to use more advertising channels that were previously cost prohibitive. The project mathematically proved that traditional advertising still plays a key role, yet there are much more important components of the consumer journey where brands can remove friction and provide value. We had a major win under our belts, and the agency started to pick up serious momentum.

Proving the New Advertising Model

Most of our initial assignments were focused on research and strategy. They were good opportunities, but not what we were passionate about. We didn't want to simply identify opportunities—we wanted to test out our new theories about building brands through empowerment and authenticity. We soon found the opportunity in Suzuki, which made some of the industry's best motorcycles but was having trouble making an emotional connection with customers.

I've been fascinated with motorcycles since childhood and motorcycles are an ideal category for our philosophy. They're not a cheap impulse buy. They're not simply transportation. They are a core part of a rider's identity. Bikers go on a lengthy journey during the purchase process. They have numerous emotional and functional needs that we could fulfill through our new vision of empowering content. We started with a web development gig and grew to become Suzuki's agency of record. Finally, we had a client ready to apply our philosophy of building brands through empowerment.

The breakthrough came on a motorcycle called the Hayabusa. It was, and still is, one of the most badass bikes on the planet. Before we committed to pursuing Suzuki's target market, we drew on every tool at our fingertips: qualitative research, quantitative research, social listening, media analytics, behavioral analytics, and more. We analyzed hundreds of thousands of data points. Perhaps most importantly, we fully immersed ourselves in the brand by sending our team to every possible place people discuss motorcycles. We talked to fans at motorcycle races, bikers at bars, enthusiasts at rallies, customizers in their shops.

The research confirmed something really interesting: Many of Busa's biggest fans weren't only focused on functional performance. They had an emotional connection to the bike. They made it part of their lifestyle, often by adding elaborate customizations. My favorite looked like the alien from *Predator.*

The challenge for us was to figure out what was at the core of the emotional connection. We dove deeper into the data and the brand immersion and found that the Hayabusa had become an organic part of hip-hop culture. Hip-hop artists were making songs and videos about the bike and sharing them online. We realized we had our killer insight for building an empowering platform. We could take a key behavior and create scale. Our goal wasn't simply to create a campaign; it was to launch a movement.

I'm certainly not cool enough to know any underground hip-hop artists, but people on our team did. They had the connections to tap into the underground scene and build an authentic, emotional connection. We reached out to about a dozen of the top underground artists in the world. For example, one was a rapper named Chali 2na, who had both underground and mainstream success, including hits with Jurassic 5, Ozomatli, and the Dave Matthews Band.

We asked each artist to create hip-hop backing tracks without lyrics. Because they were some of the best in the business, the music that came back was incredible and provided the foundation for a rap contest we called Busa Beats. The idea was that people could go to the website to browse the backing tracks and pick one or more to rap over. Using technology built by our team, fans could record their voices over those tracks to make their own raps about the bike. We also included editing tools to make sure they were satisfied with their performance before submitting.

We gave our rappers an incentive to promote their work on social media—whoever got the most votes would win a Hayabusa designed by one of the leading cycle customizers. We held an amazing photo shoot of the bike in Times Square. Rather than pay for permits, we gave a New York City cop tickets to the launch party so he would allow us to conduct a free shoot.

The next key step was turning our audience into a customized media channel. Contestants were stoked to win the customized bike and reached out on all of their social media platforms to promote their songs. With contestants having hundreds of friends on their social channels and tens of thousands one layer deeper in their social graph, we immediately drove hundreds of thousands of people to visit the site, listen to these incredible raps, and vote on their favorites. Millions of minutes were invested by fans as the contest went viral.

The platform carried the brand message far better than Suzuki ever could with traditional advertising. Rather than use a traditional ad to interrupt the audience and proclaim how great the bike is, we let the audience do it with emotional, immersive, authentic content. With a relatively tiny budget, we created content that was so powerful that it didn't need to interrupt people. Instead, our audience went out of their way to listen to the raps and share them with each other.

The contest was planned as a one-time event, but Suzuki asked us to do it again after seeing the metrics. The second year it got even bigger as the buzz spread. By the third year, we got approached by Michael Jordan's motorcycle racing team, which didn't have as much visibility as Jordan wanted. They said they would sponsor the Busa contest. Rather than the traditional advertising model, where brands spend millions getting a superstar like Jordan to endorse a product, everything became inverted. We didn't have to pitch Jordan or pay him millions for an endorsement deal. His team pitched us. We even used his famous Jumpman logo on that year's customized bike, and he opened up his Rolodex to top-tier influencers.

With Michael Jordan's cross-promotion, the contest exploded in popularity. Suzuki saw its Busa sales go up by an astounding 45 percent in a category where a 4 percent sales increase is considered dramatic. The guy who won the initial contest launched his own recording career, performing up and down the California coast. Tens of thousands of fans in his audiences were jumping up and down, rapping along with him about the Hayabusa. We love digital's ability to provide measurable results, but how can you even measure that kind of word of mouth?

We had successfully shifted the advertising model. Instead of investing a ton of Suzuki's money in TV spots and web banners, interrupting people over and over, we reached a much bigger, much more engaged audience for a fraction of the cost. We used immersive content to inform and inspire. We empowered a small audience and turned them into digitally-enabled brand evangelists. We confirmed that social media can be incredibly powerful if used properly—not as simply another place to put ads, but as a way to facilitate the spread of empowering content that people *want* to share.

How to Blow $10 Million in 60 Seconds

This was still in the early days of widespread broadband and social media. We thought we were on the verge of an empowerment revolution for the entire industry, and things would never be the same again. Instead, we found that the institutional insanity of the advertising industry would be extremely hard to shake off. Despite the growing evidence about the power of empowerment, brands remain addicted to traditional techniques.

Let's juxtapose the Busa Beats example against the approach used in a similar industry. It took place on the biggest night of the year for traditional advertising—the night that puts our most creative work in front of the biggest possible audience. Advertising people treat the Super Bowl as a sacred annual ritual. We refill our plates and drinks during the touchdown drives so we won't miss any of the commercials.

As I started work on this book, I sat down along with 100 million Americans to watch the Chiefs beat the 49ers in Super Bowl LIV. Over the course of four hours, our TVs showed dozens of commercials with dazzling visual effects, celebrity cameos, iconic pop music, and clever writing.

The consensus the next day, when the pundits had chimed in, was that Jeep had the best spot of the night: a reenactment of *Groundhog Day* starring Bill Murray. It was funny and heartwarming, and perfectly timed since Super Bowl Sunday actually fell on Groundhog Day. The commercial for the Jeep Gladiator drew thousands of tweets and hundreds of thousands of rewatches on YouTube.

As it happens, I was in the market for a new car, so the next day I started on the journey of a potential Gladiator owner. I went to sites like CarAndDriver.com and Cars .com, comparing the Gladiator with similar models. I read customer reviews and expert reviews. I attempted to find information on Jeep's website, but it turned out that was the one place Jeep definitely didn't invest much. The Gladiator was hard to find on Jeep.com, the visuals were unimpressive, and there wasn't much functional content to explain what actually made it different or better than other SUVs. The site felt completely disconnected from the hoopla of the Super Bowl commercial, as if it was run by a different team. On social media, Jeep's platforms primarily reran the commercial. They didn't continue the story in a meaningful way that let me know more about the car. I started my journey mildly curious and ended it completely frustrated.

Jeep didn't disclose how much it spent on that commercial, but let's take a ballpark guess. A Super Bowl 30-second spot costs about $3 million just for the placement, and this one ran 60 seconds. Add in the costs for filming, editing, licensing the movie rights, paying the cast (Ned Ryerson!), the crew, the ad agency, and a seven-figure fee for Bill, and we're looking at $10 to $15 million.

I salivate at that magnitude of budget. Jeep could have used that money to hire my entire agency for a full year. Or 100 recent Harvard graduates for a full year. Or it could have bought over 5 billion impressions on Twitter, 10 million targeted clicks on Google, or a year's worth of world-class content on its website. More importantly, it could have used a combination of those tools to tell a cohesive story that not only built awareness but also moved me along my journey. Instead, Jeep blew the budget by interrupting 100 million people, many of whom probably missed the commercial because they were half-drunk, in the bathroom, scarfing chicken wings, scrolling social media, and/or discussing the actual football game.

I'm not trying to pick on Jeep. To be fair, its creative team hit a home run, and it was smarter than all the other brands that wasted even more millions on *much* worse, *much* less impactful commercials. My point is that the whole system is broken, and the data that proves it is right at our fingertips. *Ad Age* devotes its entire magazine and website to Super Bowl advertising coverage, and I must admit that I love to read about the creativity and story-telling. But it also ran an article that stated in all capital letters: "80% OF SUPER BOWL ADS DON'T HELP SALES." In an industry where virtually every micro behavior can be tracked, there's no reason to invest millions in a tool that has only a 20 percent success rate.

The leaders of the advertising industry were trained to use tools that worked for a century but have been completely disrupted. Now they seem unable or unwilling to do anything differently. It's institutional insanity.

Digital Alone Is Not Enough

Many people thought digital advertising would solve the problems of institutional insanity, but shifting to digital is not enough. To understand why, let's look at J.Crew, which I know well as a former customer, not just as an ad guy.

The company began making clothing in 1947, adopted the J.Crew name in 1983, and opened its first retail store in 1989. In the early 2000s, under the leadership of Mickey Drexler and Jenna Lyons, two of the smartest executives on the planet, J.Crew turned mainstream men's clothing into a lifestyle brand. For years, I bought almost all of my clothes there.

While nobody would praise me for being uniquely dressed, J.Crew was a great resource. Like millions of other shoppers, I could pop in for some button-down shirts, a blazer, or a pair of jeans, and I'd feel confident anywhere from the office to a weekend party. Jenna was brilliant about creating a story across the entire customer experience. Unlike rivals such as the Gap and Banana Republic, she invested heavily in the granular details that sent vital, subconscious emotional triggers to shoppers, such as the quality of the lighting fixtures throughout the store. The totality of the experience told the brand story.

Then in 2017, Mickey and Jenna were pushed out by a private equity firm that had taken over the company. They were concerned that J.Crew's leadership didn't understand digital. Big mistake. The new management team understood the tools, but not the overall experience or brand identity. As J.Crew began sending more and more email blasts and following me around the web with more and more banner ads, I found myself buying less and less from the company. I started to get at least one email every day about some new offer: 10% off, 20% off, 40% off, today only, this week only, sale, sale, sale. Instead of popping in whenever I walked by a J.Crew store, I was afraid to buy. What if I paid full price for a sweater today and got an email with 40 percent off tomorrow? I'd feel like a moron.

As a marketer, I totally understood the tactics. Email blasts are virtually free, and some 26-year-old marketing manager was probably bragging about the great metrics for the campaigns. They almost certainly had the strongest return on investment of any of their marketing tactics, which allowed the brand to offer deep discounts via email. But the overall damage to the brand was catastrophic. For years, J.Crew had been an aspirational brand. Now, all of a sudden, it was a discounter only fit for bargain hunters.

Rather than empowering customers, the new approach created friction. The data showed conversions, but data are just numbers measured at a single moment. J.Crew needed insights, which combine disparate data points with a deep understanding of customers' needs. Mickey and Jenna surely would have understood that flooding people with discount emails might be cheap and powerful in the short term, but over time it would hurt the brand. When Covid-19 triggered a recession in the spring of 2020, discount shoppers abandoned retailers that they didn't feel emotionally connected to, and J.Crew had to file for Chapter 11 bankruptcy. While many may blame that outcome on the pandemic, other retailers like Restoration Hardware, who built their entire models around empowerment, doubled their market cap during the same time period.

Modern Advertising Is a Value Exchange

After two decades of taking a pragmatic look at the analytics of what works and what doesn't, it's clear that modern marketing is simply a value exchange. Brands provide customers with empowerment in the form of meaningful content and experiences, and customers respond by giving their time, data, attention, and evangelism. The key to exponential growth is actually *being* great, not *saying* you're great. Behavior over messaging. Authenticity over image.

Thinking about marketing as a value exchange shifts brands away from lazily extending traditional campaigns online. It moves them away from the social media memes that strive for irrelevant engagement metrics. It helps them avoid releasing videos that desperately seek to go viral and websites that treat every customer the same way.

Advertising still has a core role in generating traffic at the top of the funnel. Creating an empowering experience without advertising to build awareness is like building a candy store in the desert. But advertising no longer needs to tell the complete brand story; it needs to be a gateway to immersive experiences. For the Busa Beats campaign, we used traditional advertising to build awareness, but it was in the service of the larger, empowering campaign. By comparison, Jeep used it to build buzz for the Gladiator but didn't follow up with meaningful content across the journey.

The concept of a value exchange enables brands to build relationships on a one-to-one basis, moving people's lives forward with every touchpoint. Millions of consumers want to connect with brands that can help them solve their challenges. A simple shift in mindset enables brands to make strategic decisions for optimizing budgets, leveraging data, and telling meaningful brand stories. None of this is rocket science, but corporate structures are slow to change. That's one of the key reasons so many of the most successful brands are relatively young. They're not hamstrung by legacy organizational models.

More than anything, I've learned that the first and most important step for brands is to decide whether they want to break the pattern of fighting for incremental improvements and shift to a more challenging, unchartered approach that can, in fact, lead to exponential results.

It's not easy. In fact, it's hard as hell. There aren't decades of historical mathematical models. But making the conscious decision to go for it is the critical step. That one simple decision will drive every discussion and decision brands make going forward. It will create a new, clearer lens through which they look at every opportunity. And it will ensure that they are driving the revolution rather than being disrupted by it.

Three Exponential Takeaways

- Traditional advertising still works, but we are asking it to do too much. Brands need to use digital and social media to provide content that educates, informs, and inspires.

- The key to success for emotional brands is that they provide positive ROI at every touchpoint where they interact with customers. They don't only rely on traditional advertising to create their entire brand story.

- Marketers keep making ads, and the audience keeps running away. It's institutionalized muscle memory. The leaders of the advertising industry were trained to use a tool that worked for a century before it was completely disrupted.

And One Question to Ponder

Are you fighting every day for incremental results
that lead to transactional relationships with
customers, or fundamental changes that lead to
emotional relationships with customers?

Understanding the human brain isn't just a scientific issue. It's an economic imperative.

3 This Is Your Brain on Advertising

The doctor who rushed to the scene didn't believe the story until Phineas Gage leaned over in his rocking chair and puked a cup of his own brains onto the porch floor.

It was a crisp autumn afternoon in Vermont in 1848. Just a few hours before the doctor's arrival, Phineas had been a strong, intelligent, energetic man. A natural leader, he'd risen quickly through the ranks of construction crews, and by his mid-twenties he was the head of a team that built roadbeds.

That day, Phineas had been boring a deep hole in a rock. He filled it with explosives and packed the top with sand using an eight-foot-long tamping iron. He got distracted for a moment, and the iron sparked against the rock. The powder exploded. The tamping iron was propelled from the hole and into the left side of his face. It passed behind his left eye and exited out the top of his skull with such force that it landed point-first, like a javelin, 80 feet away. It was covered with his brains and blood.

Amazingly, Phineas did not die. In fact, he was conscious and alert when his crew brought him out of the hills into town for help. When the doctor came, he was sitting in front of his hotel, greeting friends and telling them the tale.

Phineas lost another ounce of his brain during surgery, but he fought through and recovered. Soon after, however, his friends and family noticed that he wasn't the same man. His intelligence and memory remained intact, but his affable personality had changed. Now he was impatient, short-fused, and aggressive. He went from a leader of men to being virtually unemployable. The rod had not only scarred his face; it had fundamentally altered his personality.

Phineas's case turned out to be a seminal moment for the scientific community. It confirmed that the human brain has different regions that perform specific functions. His intellect was fine after his injury, but his personality was not. Half a century later, the findings from this gruesome incident have never had stronger implications.

We Are in the Business of Manipulating Brains

My father, the salesman who spent his evenings showing us marketing experiments, was only part of my education about advertising. My mother also spent her life studying how to influence people's thoughts and behaviors. She was a shrink who started her own clinic when I was still an infant, using cutting-edge technology in her practice.

Just when personal computers hit the marketplace in the 1980s, she used a primitive Commodore 64 for bio-feedback, measuring how the human body responds to stress or other emotions. She measured galvanic skin response and electroencephalography by connecting the computer to sensors on a patient's fingers, wrists, and forehead to measure how they physiologically responded to stress and other stimuli. I used the equipment for my eighth-grade science fair and have remained curious about brain science and stories like the one about Phineas Gage ever since.

In recent decades, scientists have learned more about the human brain than they had in the entirety of previous human existence. Understanding that knowledge is essential for anyone trying to build an exponential brand today. As marketers, it's our job to manipulate the human brain. This may sound nefarious, but it's not. We are in the profession of creating influence and demand. That begins and ends in the brain.

This is especially important today because the fundamental structure of business value has been completely inverted. Economist Colin Mayer brilliantly uncovered that 40 years ago, 80 percent of the market value of US corporations was contained in tangible assets, such as buildings and machinery. Today, 85 percent of corporate value is based on intangibles, such as intellectual property and brand equity. All of that value exists solely in people's minds. As a result, understanding the human brain isn't just a scientific issue, it's an economic imperative.

Market capitalization is no longer based on materials that we can hold in our hands, but in concepts that we hold in our heads. Brands are constructs of our collective minds, and they are worth trillions of dollars.

We can't talk about brands or business without understanding the human brain and how it processes perceptions and manages behavior. Everything we experience on this planet happens through the brain. Every interaction with every brand is filtered and interpreted by different parts of the brain.

A good way to wrap your head around this is to consider an old philosophical question: If a tree falls in the woods and there's no one around to hear it, does it make a sound?

Scientifically speaking, the answer is no. The falling tree creates energy in the form of waves, but those waves don't turn into sound until they hit the ear of a living organism and pass through tiny bones and hair cells in the ear that turn them into electrical nerve impulses. When those nerve impulses reach the brain, it interprets them, assigns meaning to them, and decides if it should take action—all in a matter of milliseconds. Until that moment, the waves are arbitrary and meaningless. They are not sound until our brains tell us they are sound.

Everything we experience on this planet happens through the human brain. If we want to change perceptions and affect behavior—the core goal of advertising—we must first understand the material we're working with.

Brands Live in the Prefrontal Cortex

Why do people buy things? According to Economics 101, the answer is simple and rational. A company builds a product and charges a fair market price. Customers do some research and decide if the utility generated by the product is greater than the value of the hard-earned dollars they'd have to spend to get it. But neuroscience reveals that it's a lot more complicated than this.

Purchasing decisions are made in the prefrontal cortex, which sits behind the forehead and is much more advanced in Homo sapiens when compared to Neanderthals and earlier species. It evolved much more recently than the "lizard brain" that controls automatic functions like digestion and breathing. The sophistication of the prefrontal cortex is the main difference between human and animal brains.

Scientists have confirmed that the prefrontal cortex is also where brand preferences are established by running fMRI tests during the same experiment that my father conducted in our kitchen: the Pepsi challenge. Scientists love this study because there's a consistent "Pepsi Paradox"—most people prefer Pepsi in a blind taste test but prefer Coke when the brands are revealed. As subjects are tasting and pondering with sensors attached to their heads, their prefrontal cortexes light up. Fascinatingly, when researchers run the same study among people with damage to their prefrontal cortex, the Pepsi Paradox goes away—Pepsi wins even when the brand names are exposed.

Armed with this knowledge, it seems obvious that marketers just need to get access to the prefrontal cortex. The challenge is that the rest of the brain has set up sophisticated walls and roadblocks to keep information about products and brands out. Humans have a cognitive spam filter.

Our Cognitive Spam Filters

Let's take stock of the brain for a moment, because it's arguably the most complicated object known to humanity: 100 billion neurons and 50 trillion support cells, all linked together with 200,000 miles of wiring to form a network of trillions of connections. It has evolved over millions of years with one primary goal: survival. At any moment, our ancient ancestors were bombarded with millions of bits of information in our environments. Those that survived and reproduced were the ones who got good at ignoring distractions—and homed in on predators. They were able to do this thanks to something scientists call our "attentional filter."

For the most part, we modern humans don't have predators trying to kill us, but we now take in more than five times as much information as we did only 30 years ago, consuming the equivalent of over 200 newspapers daily.

The human body sends 11 million bits of data per second to the brain for processing, yet the conscious mind is able to handle less than 50 bits per second. Our attentional filters are working overtime, which means that breaking through is a tougher job than ever before.

The key to doing so is to create signals, not noise. Distractions are noise. Wasted time is noise. Pop-up ads are noise. Flo from the Progressive ads? She is noise. Unless you have the billions of dollars required to bludgeon your way through those attentional filters, your superficial messages are just noise.

Most of the time filtering out the noise is a subconscious process carried out by several different parts of the brain: the thalamus, amygdala, and basal ganglia, among others. They collaborate to filter the nonstop barrage of information that would otherwise completely incapacitate us. Millions of neurons are constantly monitoring our environment to distinguish what's an important signal and what's simply noise.

Right now, for example, you might be subconsciously hearing little sounds like squeaking seats or cars driving by your home. But you ignore nearly all of those sounds, thanks to the cognitive spam filter. Only a few succeed in breaking through to your prefrontal cortex for conscious awareness, followed perhaps by interest and action.

We can see attentional filters in action in a series of brilliant marketing messages created by an organization called Transport for London. The purpose of these ads is to motivate drivers to pay better attention to cyclists and pedestrians. To do so, Transport for London created a 60-second advertisement that opens with the line "This is an awareness test." The viewer knows that they're being tested and that a trick is coming.

In one video, there are two four-person teams passing a basketball, one dressed in white and one dressed in black. The narrator asks the viewer to count how many passes are made by the white team. It's not a difficult challenge, and most people successfully count 13 passes.

Then, the narrator asks, "But did you see the moon-walking bear?" The ad is then reshown in slow motion to highlight that a man dressed in a goofy bear costume does, in fact, moonwalk across the screen. The bear isn't on the screen for a brief moment, either. He is smack in the middle of it for the majority of the video. The video is based on an earlier experiment by Christopher Chabris and Daniel Simons, which Simons succinctly describes by saying, "Looking is not the same as seeing."

In another video, "WhoDunnIt," Transport for London alerts viewers with the same line, "This is an awareness test." The video is styled to look like a scene from an Agatha Christie mystery. The viewer sees a detective, a police officer, and three suspects are asked to solve the crime. After each suspect answers a few brief questions from the detective, one of them is revealed as the murderer and arrested. Next, viewers are asked if they noticed any changes while the camera was rolling, which almost no one does. However, it turns out that the filmmakers had made 21 different changes to the scene in the course of the video, including swapping out the weapons in the suspect's hands and even replacing the actor playing the murder victim on the floor.

Like the moonwalking bear video, viewers miss the changes because they're focusing on the clues that might solve the mystery. Even though they've been alerted to the fact that something might happen, they miss the outlandish events taking place right in front of their faces.

It's ironic that these marketing messages were used to demonstrate the power of cognitive filters, because it's these filters that create an almost insurmountable barrier for brands. Data shows that traditional advertising techniques are becoming increasingly ineffective.

It's easy to call the industry's addiction to interruptive messages insane, but the simple fact is that it's institutionalized muscle memory. Marketers are doing the same thing because that's what they know how to do. Right now for example, the business world has gone gaga over Gen Z. Even though most of them still live at home with mom, they have over $140 billion in annual spending power and will soon look like millennials, who now represent $1.4 trillion.

But this generation was raised in a connected, transparent world. Beyond their attentional filters, they have tools to avoid repetitive interruptions. Research has shown that they ignore the vast majority of TV advertisements. Not simply because they use streaming and DVRs to skip over them, but because they look down at their cell phones to avoid watching ads and only look back up when an ad segment is over. It requires virtually no effort to look away and find something more interesting.

Breaking through the Filter to Build Awareness

I'll never forget the moment I saw the greatest advertisement of all time. It smashed through my attentional filters. Yet, it didn't win any awards. It's not discussed at the annual linen-suit party the ad world throws for itself each year in the South of France. It wasn't emotional. It wasn't inspiring. It was simply a billboard.

It happened in 2001, right at the start of the digital revolution. I was driving down Route 80 outside of San Francisco, headed to a meeting. Traffic was light. I was moving at a pretty good clip, yet when I saw the ad, first my eyes and then my head spun around uncontrollably to see the future, laid out on a simple white background with a giant font: "1,000 songs in your pocket."

It was the original iPod campaign. It had a clean photo of an iPod that took up about a third of the space. The other two thirds had those five little words that anyone could understand. The ad didn't simply sell a product. It changed the world forever. MP3 players were more than a technological breakthrough. They were the foundation for smartphones, the product that fundamentally and permanently changed the relationship between brands and consumers.

Of course, that's what it looks like today. But back then, it was an entirely new category. People had no experience with it. And that made it difficult to market. No consumers understood what an MP3 player could do for them. Many other companies had already launched MP3 players, including big boys like Microsoft, Dell, and Sony. But they were all selling on tech gibberish—megabytes, gigahertz, data compression, and other esoteric concepts that had completely lost consumers.

Apple didn't offer a dramatically different product. The genius of the campaign was that Apple clearly understood where MP3 players were in the product life cycle. As a result, the ads didn't need to differentiate with emotional resonance. They didn't need a complex story. They just needed to clearly and succinctly describe what the product could do.

They offered clear and concise information. No jargon. No jingles. They explained what the product did and let the consumers' brains fill in the benefits. In print, on billboards, and on TV, the campaign shot right through attentional filters of ordinary, even technically illiterate people everywhere.

Most people in the advertising world misinterpret how Apple used advertising to help build the world's first trillion-dollar company. They focus on the iconic "1984" spot, which ran only once for 60 seconds during the 1984 Super Bowl at a then-record-breaking cost of $5 million. It depicted an Orwellian future in which a beautiful athlete hurls a sledgehammer through a screen displaying Big Brother. The tagline implies that Apple's brand-new Macintosh is a different, more exciting, flat-out cooler computer, designed for creatives and iconoclasts.

Steve Jobs loved the spot so much that he cried when talking about its creative director, Lee Clow of Chiat\Day. It won numerous awards and has been the subject of countless articles, industry awards, and presentations. It created a rallying cry for Steve and his troops. But in regard to consumer influence, it was massively overrated. The ad didn't move the needle dramatically with middle America, and it didn't make Macintosh sales explode. After the ad, Apple's share of the home PC market didn't grow significantly, and its market cap continued to hover around 3 billion dollars.

After the "1,000 Songs in Your Pocket" campaign, on the other hand, Apple grew exponentially. The company captured 74 percent of the MP3 player market and eventually morphed the iPod into iPhones. As of today, Apple has sold over 2 billion of those devices. The company's stock chart achieved the coveted hockey-stick shape, growing more than a hundredfold. A $10,000 investment in Apple's stock at the time would make you a millionaire today.

Let me be abundantly clear: Apple didn't succeed because of a single campaign. The company's recruiting, culture, product design, operations, and retail worked synergistically to create the world's largest corporation. Apple used emotional storytelling for its brand, including for iPods. But the genius of the 1,000 Songs campaign was that Apple was brave enough to be boring when it needed to be.

Boring ads may not win awards, but they can sell products. They can empower audiences. They can change companies. They can even change the world. Sometimes the bravest thing a brand can do is to be boring.

Everyone loves a great emotional ad—one that's funny, heartwarming, or inspiring. There will always be a place for emotional storytelling, and Apple continues to be one of the great brand storytellers in the world. But when every company tries to be emotional and forgets that people can come to their own conclusions about emotional benefits once they understand a product's key features, then all of the emotional stories simply become noise.

Boring ads can be a powerful tool for breaking through attentional filters. This is particularly true when products are truly differentiated. If a product is somehow better than the competition—Apple successfully placed its bets on ease of use—then the ads just need to bring those differentiating qualities to life. It is great if there can be some emotion in the story, but the emotional tail can't wag the functional dog.

Build Interest by Creating Trust

The signals that the brain uses to build awareness are electrical. They travel at 200 miles per hour on pathways between the amygdala, hippocampus, prefrontal cortex, and other areas of the brain. But electric impulses are only part of the equation for neurological functionality. The brain and body are flooded with chemicals that help facilitate the spread of these signals.

You may have a basic understanding of some of these. Dopamine, for instance, is released for the anticipation of rewards. It makes us feel good. It has been manipulated by video game and app designers to render us hopelessly addicted. The subtle buzzes, beeps, and pop-ups trigger dopamine release, making us feel subtly better and become more addicted to the games. Cortisol is another that you may have heard of. It's commonly referred to as the stress hormone. When creatures are exposed to threats, cortisol helps them focus attention and get to safety. It is released not only in the brain but also in your torso and may be the physiological phenomenon behind the concept of "gut instinct."

For brands, however, there is a chemical with a little less notoriety but much more importance: oxytocin. Neuroeconomist Paul Zak calls it "the trust chemical." Understanding oxytocin is critical for successful brand building because building trust is at the foundation of successful relationships between individuals and corporations. In consumer research, a whopping 85 percent of consumers say they will consider a brand if they trust it, but only 7 percent say they love a brand but don't trust it. Superficial messaging doesn't build trust.

Zak has spent a lifetime studying trust and its relationship with oxytocin. His initial studies were sociological in nature. He visited places ranging from remote villages to English countryside weddings carrying cases of syringes, rubber tubes, and vials to take blood samples. In each experiment, he found a direct relationship between trust and oxytocin. The more oxytocin present in the human body, the more trust existed between people.

Zak then expanded his focus to look at oxytocin's impact on financial decision-making. In one experiment, he showed different videos of the father of a boy with brain cancer and tested the amount of oxytocin that was released when people saw the video and the impact it had on the audience's likelihood to make donations. Then he took it further. In another experiment, half the viewers were first given a dose of oxytocin via nasal spray and the other half were given a placebo. Then he showed them a video asking for donations. Those who received the oxytocin spray donated, on average, 56 percent more money to the charity that had been promoted. Through these experiments, Zak demonstrated that oxytocin has a direct impact on financial behavior.

Zak recommends that brands use emotional imagery like babies and puppies in advertisements. There's nothing wrong with this advice at face value, but it's the same tactic that has been used since the dawn of multimedia messaging. It works, but it only leads to incremental results because virtually every major advertiser is using a similar technique. The real key is to build authentic trust. The formula for that is simple: honesty and transparency. Respecting time. Being clear with communications.

Brands are waking up to the importance of acting more human. They realize that all of the technology at their fingertips means that they are more than just products and advertisements. They are judged based on the totality of their behavior, including their core values and ability to demonstrate empathy.

Building trust for brands is the same as building trust for humans. Think for a moment about the people you trust. Think about the people you love. The ones you go out of your way to help. It's not simply because you enjoy their humor or are entertained by them. That's great for building a friendship, but true love is rooted in trust.

Zak and his team have found that trust can be built by simply touching people. A comforting hug, a pat on the back, or even a firm handshake can trigger the production of oxytocin. But how do we build trust in a digitally focused, no-touch world? If brands treat customers well—creating a sense of connection without physical touch—their brains will produce oxytocin and help form bonds of trust.

That's the beauty of the "1,000 Songs in Your Pocket" campaign. It builds trust by removing all complexity and obfuscation. It respects the viewer's time and attention and gives them the exact information they need, without waste or distraction.

It then became the aesthetic foundation for the brand moving forward. Recent ads still use the same clean design and messaging. Apple still avoids confusing jargon about technical specs, knowing that tech geeks can easily find those details online.

All of this consistency builds trust. The first time you see a new Apple product in one of these ads, you're subconsciously comforted by the familiar style choices. You feel confident that whatever this new gizmo does, it will be easy to use. Trust has been established.

Of course, it takes a lot more than just a clear message to create a level of trust that leads to new customers and evangelists. The process is still not complete. That takes us to the next step in the process.

Psychological Momentum Leads to Economic Outcomes

Once awareness and trust are built, the next step for brands is to influence behavior—getting people to buy products. For this step, we can shift our focus to psychology, and specifically a phenomenon known as psychological momentum. This is similar to physical momentum, which was first described by Sir Isaac Newton over 300 years ago. Try to push a 70,000-pound loaded logging truck, and it won't budge an inch. Try to stop it once it's moving, and you'll be crushed. That's the power of momentum. It's about small compounded efforts creating an exponential result.

The same is true for psychological momentum. From a physiological perspective, it's about getting the brain's neurons to fire in a synchronized way to optimize behavior and make it easy for one achievement to flow into the next. That's why psychological momentum has also been described as a "flow state" or "getting in the zone." It is common among high performers in many fields, from writing and sports to music and stock trading. If you've ever gotten into a state of relaxed focus and kept going with an activity for hours, that's psychological momentum. The same is true when you find minutes or even hours flying by while interacting with a brand's content or shopping experience.

The enemy of psychological momentum is friction, which is anything that prevents the flow state. It is the plastic packaging that requires a machete to open, the instruction manual that requires a PhD to comprehend, and the customer support phone line that leaves a caller on hold indefinitely. Fighting friction has increased in importance as the relationship between brands and consumers has become more complex. Digital friction is surprisingly common and especially frustrating, given how easily most of it could be fixed: confusing error warnings, clumsy checkout processes, websites that aren't optimized for mobile, videos that take too long to get to the point, pop-up windows that break your concentration, and dozens more stress-inducing touchpoints. We all have personal peeves.

Researchers have studied psychological momentum and the effects of friction on flow. One of the most tangible examples is demonstrated on the basketball court when coaches call time-outs when their opponents are making a run. A recent study found that when NCAA basketball teams took a time-out to break the other team's psychological momentum, the performance of the other team decreased by 56 percent. Yet, most companies keep allowing friction to break the momentum of their potential customers. That's one of the key reasons why we see $1.6 trillion worth of abandoned e-commerce shopping carts every year.

Finding friction is only half of the equation. The second half is the exciting part. It's about replacing friction with empowerment. It's about brands moving people's lives forward one small step at a time. While some brands have tackled massive issues like saving the environment or pressing social issues, the truth is that brands can generate significant value with more humble ambitions.

Returning to the Apple example, they did it by tackling the shopping experience. It's hard to imagine an industry more clogged up with friction than tech before Apple set out to completely reinvent shopping. You'd walk into Best Buy, CompUSA, or Circuit City to find haphazard, dimly lit, unpleasant aisles of boxes, with virtually no merchandising. Just ugly brown boxes stacked on top of each other. Barely a sticker to reveal what was inside.

Around the time that I almost crashed my car while checking out the "1,000 Songs" ad on Route 80, I walked into a CompUSA and saw the universe shift in one brief moment. I was on the escalator, almost to the second floor. As I rose above the brown boxes stacked on the first floor, I saw hundreds more stacked on the second. I was feeling discouraged, like everyone else in that store. But then I saw something new. It was brightly lit with shiny products. I remember feeling like I could almost hear choral singing. It was an oasis. It was merchandising.

Rather than leaving Apple products stacked in brown boxes, they took them out and put them on a clean table, with bright lights. People could see and touch the computers. It seems silly to even describe the experience because it's so obvious in retrospect. Steve Jobs saw a huge opportunity to make shopping easy and fun rather than oppressive. He knew a better retail experience could not only help drive conversions but also help build an army of brand evangelists.

Soon after, the first Apple Stores eliminated more friction and greased the wheels of psychological momentum. They featured multiple display models of every item so you could try the products for as long as you wanted before buying one. An army of young techies were waiting to help you, with no sales commissions that might give them an incentive to pressure customers. They even removed the most hated piece of friction in any store—the checkout line—by enabling those same techies to process your payment on a handheld device. Jobs knew that waiting around to give a company money sucks.

The goal of the Apple Stores wasn't just to sell products. They were designed to empower people to improve their own creativity and performance. If customers didn't understand something or needed help with a product they already owned, they could visit the Genius Bar for customized, one-on-one answers and solutions. This opened up Apple's audience to millions of customers who may have been intimidated by the switch from a PC-dominated world to Mac computers. And it helped create evangelists out of current customers who were simply looking for advice for how to get more value out of the products they owned.

Each of these small friction-fighting maneuvers built psychological momentum that compounded to generate exponential results.

The World's First Trillion-Dollar Company Simply Provided Foreshadowing

Many of the techniques employed by Apple Stores feel commonplace now. But what Apple did with the stores wasn't simply revolutionary—it was foreshadowing. It was a demonstration of the importance of managing the entire consumer journey, not just the commonplace components of telling an emotional story. It proved that effective modern marketing is about breaking through the attentional filters by leveraging the complete spectrum of neurological processes: electrical, chemical, and psychological. It's about redefining advertising from being about more than just a 30-second spot to being about every touchpoint in the consumer journey. It's about recognizing that the relationship between brands and consumers is more complex than ever and emotional storytelling is simply one small piece of the puzzle. Empowering experiences throughout the journey are critical for affecting behavior and driving revenue.

Let's take the maneuvers by Warby Parker as another example. Warby started with a $2,500 grant, performed modestly for a while, and then grew exponentially to an incredible $3 billion valuation in only 10 years. It used the same techniques that Apple did. Like Apple, it had a simple insight: glasses should be affordable. It then went to battle with Luxottica, which owned the vast majority of eyewear brands and used its market dominance to charge outrageous prices.

Like Apple, Warby uses a combination of emotional and functional content and experiences to break through filters and drive growth. Rather than rely on interruptive TV ads to try to create buzz or build an emotional connection, the brand drives word-of-mouth through a program that donates a pair of free glasses to the poor for every pair purchased. The brand has donated over 8 million pairs of glasses, creating brighter futures for deserving families around the world. Warby built trust by enabling users to try on five pairs at home before choosing one to be filled with prescription lenses.

And just like Apple's instant checkout, Warby fights friction at every point in the sales process with a proprietary point-of-sale system that creates a personalized relationship with customers across stores, websites, and email. Knowing how important frictionless commerce would be, it vetted 30 vendors before deciding to build its own proprietary system. Even Warby's next-generation approach doesn't feel cutting edge anymore. Functional and frictionless shopping is simply table stakes.

Creativity Alone Won't Improve Sales

As marketers, we don't need a PhD in brain science, but we do need a basic grasp of the drivers of human behavior. This knowledge can help us frame and sequence our messages for optimal impact. We can't be so pompous as to expect people to invest their time, energy, and cognitive capacity in trying to figure out our offerings. We need to show empathy and respect to our audience, because they're already bombarded and inundated with information all day long.

We need to make it as easy as possible for them to grasp the features and functionality of our products. We need to use simple language and uncluttered designs. We need to make details like packaging and merchandising intuitive. We need to improve the boring but essential stuff, like website functionality and customer service. Investing resources in small, methodical steps delivers a far greater return than a single big campaign.

Let's not get sucked into the cult of creativity. I love creative advertising as much as anyone, but it's just one piece of the bigger picture. Without harnessing all of the aspects of the brain, creativity alone won't improve sales—even if we win awards or get invited to drink rosé on the beaches of Cannes.

Let's not simply ask ourselves what's cool or creative. The lesson from Phineas Gage is that we need to understand the human brain so that we can create content that is meaningful and empowering enough to break through cognitive spam filters, generate trust, build psychological momentum, drive purchases, and motivate recommendations.

Three Exponential Takeaways

- Market capitalization is no longer based on materials that we can hold in our hands but in concepts that we hold in our heads. Brands are constructs of our collective minds. They can be worth billions of dollars.

- Human beings have cognitive spam filters that make it extremely difficult for interruptive messages to break through.

- There will always be a place for emotional storytelling, but the emotional tail can't wag the functional dog. When every brand is trying to be emotional, sometimes the bravest thing a brand can do is be boring.

And One Question to Ponder

Are you using your time and talent to create a modern version of spam, or are you creating content that people would actually go out of their way to enjoy?

Brands are not simply a story. They are a cognitive shortcut.

4 Your Brand Is Your Most Important Asset

It took every ounce of strength not to cry the first time I saw Harris's face. The benign tumor hung from his chin, the size of a second head. The sheer size and weight of it turned his mouth inside out, exposing red flesh where his lips once were.

There were many similar photos of people from Harris's village. Some were slowly dying because they couldn't breathe properly; others were stoned by villagers who thought they were possessed.

When Scott Harrison told Harris's story to our team, we cried when he wanted us to cry. We laughed when he wanted us to laugh. We gave when he wanted us to give. We have all seen devastating photographs of people in need. What made this experience different was that it was told by a master of influence.

Scott is the CEO of charity: water, a nonprofit whose goal is to bring clean drinking water to people in developing countries. One of the keys to his success is sharing his story with influencers in the marketing and technology industries. He came to our agency to help build awareness for his brand.

Scott has his own story of pain. When he was a young boy growing up in suburban New Jersey, the heater in his home had a carbon monoxide leak, years before carbon monoxide alarms became commonplace. His parents didn't know that poison was slowly leaking into their home. They didn't know that Scott's mother, who was home all day, was being irreparably harmed by the invisible, odorless gas. They thought she had the flu. But soon, the physical ailments grew until she was incapacitated.

They went from doctor to doctor, looking for the cure. Finally, a plumber found the problem: three pinhole-sized holes in the back of the radiator. But the damage had been done. Scott's mother would forever be allergic to the world around her. Odors and gases that others barely noticed would leave her with uncontrollable headaches, dizziness, and fatigue. Common factors such as perfume, air conditioning, car exhaust, onions, and sealant on wood floors were poisons to her.

Scott spent his childhood taking care of his mom. There were days spent outside under a lean-to, where his mom could escape the everyday odors in their home. There were days when he worked with his father to cover the walls in aluminum foil looking for a homegrown solution. There were days where he tried on his mom's carbon face mask to see what it felt like to live with a filter covering her nose and mouth all day.

Almost every day, they prayed. The Harrison home was deeply religious. They didn't sue the gas company, and they did their best to live without bitterness. They came together, united by Scott's piano playing and the daily prayer.

Once Scott graduated high school, he went in the completely opposite direction. He moved to New York City to start a band and quickly rose to the top of the NYC music scene. Soon he was playing in top venues, including the famed CBGB, before pivoting to become a nightclub promoter. Budweiser and Skyy Vodka paid him thousands just to be seen drinking their products. He had beautiful models on his arm and the world's most powerful city at his feet. He was the guy who decided which nightclubs were cool.

Scott dabbled in everything the lifestyle had to offer—sex, pornography, and virtually every drug short of heroin. Every night was spent with thousands of his closest friends. He had it all. Until he realized he didn't have anything worthwhile.

While on vacation in South America with a group of hard-partying friends from the club scene, he realized the lifestyle that he dominated wasn't for him. He needed meaning. He needed to get back to his roots.

Scott left early from the trip and called every major charitable organization he could, asking them if he could donate his time. Nobody wanted him, even for free. His résumé as a drug-consuming nightclub promoter wasn't exactly the profile they were looking for. Finally, he found Mercy Ships, which said he could join them and document the experience if Scott would pay them $500 a month to volunteer. Scott agreed. They then took him to Liberia, a place he previously couldn't even find on a map.

Scott found himself on a 500-foot ship with doctors who donated their time to patients in other countries who didn't have access to medical care. He spent time with Dr. Gary Parker, who had thought he was going for a brief trip but ended up staying for 29 years. He also met Harris and other villagers with growths the size of bowling balls protruding from their faces.

I work in an industry based on the concept of storytelling, but one in which most people are beyond terrible at it. At industry conferences, my mind typically wanders, and I barely grasp any key points. With Scott, I was riveted. Admittedly, the story had all the key ingredients: debauchery, redemption, and character development. But it was more than that. When it comes to storytelling, even some of the best can only play the notes. Scott could play the music.

When the tortured faces of the Liberians with tumors were projected on the screen, everyone felt like crying. I interrupted Scott to ask what caused them. He patiently smirked at me because he wasn't quite ready to reveal that. He was telling a story, and we were transfixed.

The cause was the water the Liberians drink. It contains both microscopic and plainly visible organisms that are harmful to human beings. Scott showed us pictures of the water and zoomed in so we could see the leeches and parasites swimming in it. He noted that he wouldn't even let his dog walk in the water that these people drank.

Scott explained that the problems that result from a lack of clean water hit women especially hard. They walk for hours to access clean water, wading into streams filled with crocodiles or digging in the sand, desperately trying to find a few ounces for their families.

Despite the massive size of the tumors, Dr. Gary and others were able to remove them and send many of the villagers home scarred but otherwise normal in appearance. They were dedicating their lives to saving these people, and Scott documented the experience with photos, videos, and stories.

During that trip, Scott had an epiphany. He found his life calling. He went back to New York City and did what he did best. He threw a party for 700 of his closest friends at a nightclub. He showed them photos of the women and children. He showed them the parasites. He told them the solution was clean water.

Almost 800 million people on this planet don't have access to clean water. This causes irreparable harm, and Scott had a solution. He would raise money for wells in Africa, East Asia, and wherever else clean water was needed. He started charity: water.

I'm fascinated by people like Scott Harrison because he is a master of influence who uses his gifts for the greater good. He laughs at himself for his once overwhelming need to make sure his Rolex watch was visible to photographers when they snapped shots of him enjoying bottle service at 3 a.m. But to me, that's the genius. He understood the power of little things, like the angle of your wrist, that could lead to incredible results.

Thankfully for millions of people around the world, Scott turned his attention away from nightclubs and toward more important things. He used his genius to create not merely a charitable organization but a global brand.

The team at charity: water obsesses about the consistency of its image. It invests in high-quality photography to illustrate the suffering caused by a lack of clean water and to show how the organization turns donations into dramatic results. It produces some of the strongest videos, posters, annual reports, and other materials I've ever seen. Its approach is not to beg for donations, but to invite donors to join an uplifting, successful movement.

I've worked with numerous charities, including both startups and behemoths. Their hearts and souls are dedicated to making the world a better place, but they often don't create an identity that can be leveraged for more than the sum of its parts. Half of all charitable organizations fail, not because they lack passion, but because they don't understand how to build a brand. charity: water, on the other hand, could teach a master class on the subject and has generated exponential results. As Scott put it, "I'm still inviting people to a party. It's just a much more redemptive one."

Quite Simply, Brands Are Cognitive Shortcuts

It was interesting to spend time with Scott because he and his wife voraciously studied marketing and branding, but they instinctively understood the concepts much better than the authors of many of the books they read. Most importantly, they understand that brand building is a methodical process based on small, compounding steps that lead to exponential results.

A brand is not some esoteric concept. It is a tangible asset that can be worth billions of dollars. The fact that people prefer Coke over Pepsi even though Pepsi typically wins blind taste tests has massive financial implications. According to Kantar, the Coca-Cola brand is worth $84 billion, more than six times as much as Pepsi. Coke is not alone. Apple's brand is worth over 600 billion dollars. Amazon's is almost 700 billion. That means that the little logo that sits on the side of their packages is worth more than the GDP of Greece.

So, what exactly is a brand? Is it a symbol? A story? A set of beliefs or values? An aggregation of behaviors? An economic model? If you scan the literature on the topic, there are thousands of theories about brands. Many of them gravitate toward the concept of a brand being a story, which is the direct outcome of a generation that grew up on the 30-second advertisement. But that's no longer correct. Quite simply, a brand is a cognitive shortcut.

In a world where humans are exposed to 5,000 brand messages per day, where the human brain consumes 11 million bits of information every minute, where well over 99 percent of information is automatically filtered by the collective mechanics of the brain, a brand is a shortcut that helps people process and understand the meaning behind the logo.

The understanding and processing of such symbols is a uniquely human capability. No other creature comes remotely close to our ability to convert symbols into meaning. People use those shapes and colors as a shortcut to understand whether or not their beliefs align with a company's core values and whether or not their unmet needs can be fulfilled by the features of its products.

Building a brand isn't a creative process mastered by people like Paul Rand, creator of some of the most iconic logos of all time, including IBM, ABC, and UPS. The logo is just the window dressing. Brand building is a methodical, scientific process that has been mastered by a small set of companies that control almost everything Americans buy.

The thousands of brands that stock the shelves of supermarkets, pharmacies, and beauty stores are owned by just a few dozen corporations. In your local Sephora, 182 beauty brands are owned by just seven holding companies. In your local supermarket, over 600 brands are owned by just 12 holding companies. Niche brands like California Pizza Kitchen, PowerBar, Taster's Choice, and Gerber probably seem completely unrelated. But they are owned by the same company: Nestlé. Niche beers like Goose Island IPA and Modelo Especial are both owned by Anheuser-Busch InBev, which now controls over half of the beer market, despite the supposedly explosive growth of microbrew beers.

These companies are absolute geniuses at identifying consumers' emotional and functional needs and building brands that fulfill them. They know exactly how to turn a good product into a great brand. And that's about a hell of a lot more than simply creating a fancy logo.

It requires a process called brand management, and companies like Procter & Gamble, Nestlé, General Mills, Coca-Cola, and Pepsi mastered it over time, largely using analytics. While the principles of brand management have been employed throughout history, often by leaders of empires, the modern version of it was the brainchild of Neil McElroy, a Harvard graduate and former US secretary of defense who worked for Procter & Gamble on the Camay brand. The problem P&G faced was that it also owned the Ivory Soap brand, which was doing well against rivals like Palmolive and Lever Brothers, but also against Camay.

McElroy drafted a memo that argued for a system for brand differentiation and brand building. A hallmark of his plan was that a team with defined roles should be responsible for building equity and capturing market share. He suggested the team should include a brand manager, a brand assistant, researchers, and a handful of other positions focused on specific tasks and activities.

He proposed an approach for segmented marketing, which enabled a brand's personality to be definitively different from the other brands in a company's brand portfolio. As a result, each brand could fight for a unique audience rather than compete against one another. Ivory and Camay could both thrive in their own separate lanes.

This methodical, differentiated approach enabled Procter & Gamble to grow exponentially by building and acquiring additional brands and brand management teams.

Over time, the company optimized the process and ultimately mastered the separate but related arts of brand building and team building.

P&G and other holding companies today have internal brand schools and strict processes for turning products into billion-dollar brands. They hire MBAs to manage the process and determine the career trajectory for thousands of people.

The process works amazingly well. In 2020, P&G took in $71 billion in revenue, with about 20 of its brands—Bounty, Gillette, and Crest among them—bringing in more than $1 billion each year.

The Traditional Process for Brand Building

Traditional brand management is rooted in a diagram known as a brand pyramid. Let's examine how it works through the lens of charity: water.

The pyramid starts with a foundational layer and then builds upward with increasingly creative layers. The first three layers—reasons to believe (RTBs), mission, and values—are internally facing and functional, largely intended to align the team. The top two—brand personality and tagline—are external facing and emotional, intended to inspire customers. Getting the sequence right from the bottom up is essential. Skipping any layer makes the pyramid unstable.

At the base of the pyramid are RTBs, which are the functional benefits that make a brand great. For charity: water, these include an embrace of transparency and authenticity. One level up from the RTBs is the mission. charity: water's mission is simple and clear: "To bring clean and safe drinking water to people in developing countries." The next layer up are the values, behaviors, and beliefs. charity: water's documented beliefs include Integrity, Respect, Excellence, Innovation, Generosity, and Passion.

With that internal-facing foundation in place, the next step up the pyramid is the brand's public personality. charity: water's personality traits are Helpful, Optimistic, Honest, Adventurous, Generous, Grateful, Creative, Respectful—all of which are interrelated and reflect an overall positive energy. Finally, a brand finds its external summary in the form of a tagline, ideally one that's emotional, inspiring, and succinct. charity: water nailed it with the tagline "Water Changes Everything."

Consistent communications bring the entire pyramid to life by reinforcing the brand's identity. charity: water has an 86-page brand book that defines every aspect of how it presents itself to the world, including everything from fonts to social media imagery. Our suspicious brains are reassured by cohesive messaging, even at the level of colors and typography.

Creating a brand pyramid is not a difficult process on the surface. It's as simple as documenting each level of a brand's identity from the reasons to believe to the final tagline. But adhering to one requires discipline that most brands don't have. Frankly, process and consistency are boring, so most brands skip this step or vacillate when new ideas, opportunities, or technologies emerge. But inconsistency crushes the effectiveness of the cognitive shortcuts and negatively impacts brand equity. Simply creating and adhering to a traditional brand pyramid is enough to put a brand into the upper echelon of its industry.

Modern Brands Are Defined by What They Do, Not What They Say

Building a successful brand isn't simply about nailing the brand pyramid anymore, because brands are no longer built based on how they are portrayed. Now, brands are built based on how they behave.

The story of Nike, a brand now worth $35 billion, highlights the difference between the old way of branding and how it has changed. Phil Knight and Bill Bowerman launched the brand with a simple insight: high-performance runners need high-performance shoes. They made their prototype soles in a waffle maker, then hired a graphic designer at the University of Oregon who created the Swoosh logo for just $2 per hour—a mere $35 fee that probably represents the strongest return on brand investment in world history.

Early on, Nike was not a flashy brand. It created a functional product that was used only by expert runners. Then in 1987, Nike invited the ad agency Wieden + Kennedy to pitch it on a new campaign. The night before the big pitch, Dan Wieden came up with Nike's legendary tagline. His team had pored through research and worked tirelessly to brainstorm ideas, but Dan still wasn't satisfied with what they planned to present. He grabbed a stiff drink and turned on his TV to relax. On the news was the execution of Gary Gilmore, who had been convicted of killing two people in Utah. Gilmore's last words before facing the firing squad were "Let's Do It." The line broke through the stress and ignited something in Dan's mind. He shifted a word and decided on an 11th-hour pivot to "Just Do It."

Since then, Nike has turned "Just Do It" into a multibillion-dollar asset. But that road has not been without its rocks. In fact, Nike almost lost it all in a moment that highlights how transparency has changed the game from the old image-based world of branding to a new world of behavior-based branding.

In 1997, Nike commissioned a confidential investigation by Ernst & Young that found atrocious conditions in the overseas factories that supplied its sneakers. For example, workers at a factory near Ho Chi Minh City were exposed to carcinogens that exceeded legal standards by 177 times. The report was leaked to the *New York Times* and then made headlines everywhere. Nike didn't own the factories. The company outsourced all of its manufacturing to vendors around the world. But consumers didn't care and held the brand responsible. As a result, the company's stock price tanked, and Nike lost 50 percent of its market cap virtually overnight.

Nike's products are just rubber, cloth, and stitching. The Swoosh, brand story, "Just Do It" slogan, and superstar endorsements create cognitive shortcuts to the company's values and its promise of integrity and quality. Suddenly, those shortcuts were telling a different story. Who wants to be associated with a brand that hurts women and children?

But here's the part of this story that I love: Nike changed. Whether it was a moral awakening or a purely financial decision doesn't really matter. What matters is that the company completely overhauled its supply chain. In 2005, Nike embraced transparency and released a global database of more than 700 factories. This wasn't required by law; it was a proactive step that signaled a dramatic shift from the brand's previously opaque supply chain. Nike took a leadership position in ethical outsourcing. Soon, Timberland, Puma, Adidas, and Reebok followed the brand's lead, ultimately shining a light on their supply chains and the treatment of their global workforce. Environmental impact statements soon followed. Nike's brand and financial value recovered and then grew exponentially, proving that you can't use PR or advertising to get past a brand crisis—you actually have to change your behavior.

Nike also proved that successful branding in the age of transparency isn't simply about strong ethical behavior; it's about marketing with a point of view. In 2018, the brand ran ads supporting Colin Kaepernick, the San Francisco 49ers quarterback who was the first professional sports player to protest racism by taking a knee during the national anthem before games—and consequently found himself without a job, shut out of the league. Those ads, which featured the stirring tagline "Believe in something, even if it means sacrificing everything" stirred up as much controversy as Kaepernick himself.

Nike lost about $3.5 billion in market cap in the immediate backlash from its Kaepernick endorsement. Media pundits declared that the brand would suffer severe long-term damage. But its core audience—younger, more diverse, more progressive—quickly rewarded Nike for demonstrating bravery and supporting racial equality. Within weeks, Nike's stock had more than rebounded.

The risk paid off because brands don't need to please everyone. They need to be true to their values and core audience. Nike's market cap is now twice as high as when the Kaepernick ad came out and seven times higher than when the brand started to clean up its supply chain. Brand behavior and marketing with a point of view break through the enemy of incrementalism.

People Want More Than Cool Products and Clever Taglines

Now that people can see the totality of any company's behavior, many only want to support those whose values truly align with their own. This is particularly true of younger consumers, who have been raised in a transparent world. Surveys show that 83 percent of them want companies to align with them on values and social issues; 65 percent would consider boycotting a company that holds views in conflict with their own beliefs; 55 percent are willing to pay more for products or services from companies that are committed to positive social and environmental impact.

What Nike learned the hard way, Scott Harrison knew intuitively: Trust follows transparency. He found a powerful insight in an arresting data point: 42 percent of people don't trust charities. That is a massive problem, but Scott knew he could turn it into an advantage if he could create transparency. Even though Scott had been a master of spin as a nightclub promoter, he knew that charity: water did not have the luxury of spin. It couldn't just claim to be great, it had to actually *be* great. So, he devised a number of ways to make it easy for potential donors to trust the organization.

For example, he installed a GPS tracker into every well the charity dug so that donors could find the exact spot where their dollars were helping people. He persuaded a group of philanthropists to underwrite the organization's overhead, salaries, and marketing costs so that 100 percent of every regular donation goes directly to providing clean water. This unique arrangement eliminated one of the biggest fears people have about charities: that they are paying for salaries and overhead rather than helping as many people as possible.

Scott then leveraged creativity and technology to change the entire model for donations. Rather than simply asking people to donate, he created a platform that enabled them to work together with their friends to generate donations. At first, people used their birthdays to reach out. For example, when people turned 40, they used a simple tool that enabled everyone to donate $40. Donors then took it to the next level and found some really cool ways to raise money. A guy named David raffled off his face and let the winner decide how he would shave his beard. A young girl ate only beans for a month. A woman swam naked across San Francisco Bay. The audience wasn't simply inspired—they were empowered. Millions upon millions of dollars were raised.

Shifting from Brand Pyramids to Brand Building

The traditional marketing process still works in categories like soap and toothpaste, where a small increase in market share can translate into millions of dollars in extra revenue. But exponential brands are outperforming those traditional brands by focusing on what they do, not what they say. They're finding smarter ways to bypass the brain's filters, embrace transparency, and live up to a higher purpose. Then they're developing immersive, empowering content to bring that purpose to life.

To participate in this revolutionary approach, brands need to augment the brand pyramid with an approach that drives changes in brand behavior that are commensurate with changes in consumer behavior. Let's call it a brand building instead of a brand pyramid. That building needs a strong foundation to keep the structure upright, solid pillars to create the frame, and an appealing exterior to attract attention.

The foundation of this building is built on empathy and empowerment. Empathy is about listening to your audience and understanding what they really want. It's about using the unprecedented data at our fingertips to go beyond demographic research and identify the unmet emotional and functional needs of customers. Empathy turns insights into opportunities. Empathy enabled charity: water to understand the huge proportion of people who don't trust charities. Great brands are empathetic. Great brands start with great listening.

Empowerment, on the other hand, is about turning that empathy into action. It's about ensuring that a brand is rooted in improving people's lives, one small step at a time. charity: water empowers millions of people by giving them proof that their donations aren't being wasted and making it easy to amplify their impact through technology-fueled fundraisers. Empowerment requires a shift away from projecting an image to creating meaningful experiences that positively affect people's lives. It's about investing in being great, not simply saying you're great.

Above the foundation are three key pillars: inspiration, aspiration, and education. Inspiration is at the core of every exponential brand we've discussed so far. They help us envision a better version of ourselves and empower us with tools to make it happen. Apple inspires us to be more creative. Nike inspires us to be more athletic. charity: water inspires us to be generous.

The difference between inspiration and aspiration is subtle but profound. Inspiration is about motivating someone to do more: to be more creative, more athletic, more charitable. Aspiration is about showing them the destination of that activity. Apple shows artists creating groundbreaking work. Nike shows us athletes flying through the air. charity: water uses beautiful photographs of water gushing out across the dry African plains. Aspiration helps us hope, dream, and visualize how we can be better tomorrow than we are today.

The third pillar, education, may be the least exciting but most important of all. Education turns inspiration and aspiration into reality, giving the audience practical tools and information to help them reach their goals. For Apple, it's the Genius Bar in each retail store, teaching people how to get the most out of their products. For Nike, it's apps and videos that help people become more fit or more skilled in their favorite sport. For charity: water, it's online content that explains the hidden tragedy of dirty water and how to fix it. Education can be powerful at both a macro level by addressing issues that affect people in the totality of an industry and at a micro level by helping people understand the features and functions of a product. It can be as quick as an Instagram photo or as deep as a long-form video series. The key is to provide demonstrable value.

The exterior of the building is based in transparency and simplicity. As we've seen throughout this book, transparency is now inevitable—the only question is whether a brand hides from it or embraces it. Consumers today see right through any attempt at obfuscation, duplicity, or superficial messaging. Brands must find the nexus of what they stand for and what their audiences really care about. Nike succeeded by cleaning up its supply chain and helping its competitors do the same. charity: water succeeded by providing technology that enabled donors to see exactly where their dollars were going.

The other part of our new brand building's exterior is simplicity. Even the most beloved brands and the most appealing products will suffer if there's friction during the shopping process. If people can't find the information they need—ratings, reviews, features, technical specs—or if they can't easily complete a purchase without jumping through frustrating hoops, they will be lost. Maybe forever. Research shows that brands that don't provide simple experiences lose over $80 billion in potential transactions. The competition is always one click away. Brand purpose may create interest and momentum, but friction can create an insurmountable barrier.

When you put it all together, our new brand building gives people both emotionally satisfying and intellectually appealing reasons to make the journey from prospect to customer, and then from customer to evangelist. The brand pyramid will always be a powerful tool for creating a brand identity, but the brand building is what drives exponential results.

Building Brand Equity Requires Investments and Patience

Most advertising, whether using an old or new medium, can typically be broken down into two categories: direct response and brand building. Direct response includes junk mail, infomercials, old-fashioned newspaper ads, and cold calls that interrupt dinner. It's messages that scream, "Act now!" or "Supplies are running out!" It's social media posts and web banners with "Buy Now!" buttons.

Experts in direct response use sophisticated mathematical formulas to ensure that they maximize profits from their advertising investments. When direct response is done well, companies can scale up aggressively because every dollar invested adds a predictable profit. Chief financial officers love it because it's easy to make a positive cost/benefit analysis of any expenditure.

The problem with direct response advertising is that performance remains linear, at best. Brands need to continuously invest in "Buy Now" techniques, which don't create a compounding effect and don't produce brand evangelists. Every customer must be won again for every transaction. Even worse, direct response advertising leaves companies vulnerable to competition. It generates demand, but it doesn't create any affection for the brand. In fact, the opposite is often true. For every person who makes a purchase through a direct response ad, there may be thousands who ignore it or get annoyed. Think about how you feel when you get junk mail in your mailbox or pop-up banners on a website. Do they make you more likely to buy from a brand, or less?

Brand advertising is fundamentally different. It's not trying to get you to "Buy Now!" It explains what a brand stands for and what makes it different. It's the difference between "2-for-1 sneaker sale, this week only!" and "Just Do It." Nike's inspiring videos of superstar and amateur athletes capture mindshare, which eventually leads to market share.

Like the proverbial high road that is harder to get to and takes you to a better place, brand advertising takes time, creativity, alignment, and patience. It follows an exponential curve that takes longer to establish but eventually grows dramatically. It generates billions in equity that can't easily be replaced.

The challenge lies in the word "eventually." If you make a graph that charts investments and profit, growth will start out relatively flat with little or no return on investment. As branding efforts create meaning and spark conversations with target audiences, performance will eventually point skyward. Patient investors and management teams know that most superstar brands initially require lots of time and investment before they take off.

The problem is that corporations lose patience and nerve. Chief marketing officers at the world's largest advertisers have an average tenure of 41 months, a number that has been steadily decreasing. By comparison, the average CEO has a tenure of over 10 years. The short shelf life of marketing executives forces short-term thinking and inconsistent brand identities. One of the reasons Nike is so successful is that the company has stuck with "Just Do It" for over three decades, an absolute rarity in the world of brand building.

As Scott explained to me about his approach with charity: water, "I've heard that some of the big charities have tested banner ads of the kid with flies on his face, turning in slow motion to the camera. Their image is going to outperform and raise more money. But I believe that's damaging to their brands in the long term. I want our brand to stand for a smiling child getting clean water, because we are making progress and moving in this direction towards a world where everyone has clean water."

Ultimately, brand advertising drives brand equity—the influence a brand name has in the minds of consumers. Brand equity is built through the totality of a brand's behavior, both positive and negative. It holds massive financial value because it translates to revenue-generating behaviors, including repeat purchases, reduced price sensitivity, and evangelism. Exponential brands have the patience to resist the quick fix of direct response and invest in long-term brand equity. Most importantly, they treat brand building with the appropriate reverence and processes, because a brand is a company's most valuable asset.

Three Exponential Takeaways

- A brand is a company's most important asset. Some are worth more than the GDP of major nations.

- A brand pyramid is a classic way to develop a brand's identity, and just developing one can create a competitive advantage.

- While brand pyramids provide a nice foundation, the model should be modernized to put an emphasis on behavior over messaging. It requires a commitment to empathy, empowerment, and transparency.

And One Question to Ponder

Given that a brand is your business's most valuable asset, are you sure your team and your target audience fully understand what your brand stands for?

Brands no longer need
to bludgeon people with
repeated interruptions.
They can create
meaningful content for
every step of the modern
consumer journey.

5 Leveraging the Consumer Journey

When Gino Greganti went to war in Afghanistan, he felt like a hero. When he came home, he felt like a zero.

He was a classic Marine: tall, lean, and handsome. Just after arriving at Camp Rhino, the first US base established in Afghanistan, Gino and two others were pinned down on the roof of a building by Taliban gunfire. A Huey Cobra helicopter took off about 200 yards away and, after taking heavy fire, exploded in midair. Chaos ensued. Gino could hear bullets whizzing past his head as he crouched behind a wall for hours, his adrenaline flowing uncontrollably. A few months later, when he returned from Afghanistan, Gino suffered from post-traumatic stress disorder (PTSD) and chronic feelings of worthlessness. The Marines taught him how to fight, but not how to come home.

Gino went from veterans hospital to veterans hospital looking for a cure. Prescription drugs only made him feel disconnected from the world around him. Meditation didn't help. His thoughts turned to suicide, which seemed like the only way to ease his pain. Gino was far from alone in his suffering. It's been reported that one in three returning troops are now diagnosed with PTSD, two out of three of their marriages fail, and twenty-two of them commit suicide every day.

While he was waiting at a veterans hospital one day, a social worker with a clipboard walked in and said, "I don't normally do this, but do you mind if I give you a hug? You look like you need a hug." He paused, not sure how to reply, his face blank.

When he murmured "Sure," she wrapped her arms around him for a hug and told him, "I'm a vet too. I was a nurse in the Gulf War, and I have PTSD. I've been through this, and you're going to be okay. You're not okay now, but you're gonna be okay. You just have to keep going forward."

Gino started to cry uncontrollably from sheer relief. He had finally found someone who felt his pain. "I completely broke down emotionally," he later told me. "That's all I needed. Someone to tell me I wasn't crazy."

That night, he and his wife watched a video on Facebook about another veteran who had also discovered the power of a hug. Like Gino, this Marine had seen terrible things in war and struggled with pharmacology, therapy, and suicidal thoughts. He had a succinct explanation of the problem: "It's a hard thing when you're taught how to fear and hate and go to war, but you forget how to love." He tattooed

"HUMAN" across his back and was traveling across the country giving hugs to help his fellow veterans.

Gino was riveted by the video and shocked to discover that the traveling hugger was a former Marine buddy named Ian Michael. Soon Ian and Gino reconnected and made plans to help other traumatized veterans, not just from Afghanistan but any war. They planned to start small, by going to one veterans hospital with a sign that said "Hug a Vet." If it worked, they planned to travel around the country giving free hugs to anyone who would accept them.

It took a few tries before they worked up the courage to finally enter the hospital and hug other veterans. When they did, they were greeted by an administrator who had, by coincidence, done a college project giving hugs to people in need. She allowed them in. By the end of that day, the administrator told them that she had never seen so much positivity or heard so much laughter in the hospital. She asked Ian and Gino to return. And so began the Human Hug Project, a grassroots organization determined to bring awareness to the PTSD crisis by giving love back to humanity, one hug at a time.

A Brand with a Story to Tell

Around the same time, my firm was working with Super 8 by Wyndham, an economy hotel brand confronting a significant challenge. The chain's leadership decided to elevate the brand and started by improving the product. They redesigned and renovated Super 8 rooms, adding distinctive touches like framed black-and-white photography that gave local flavor. The rooms got new bedding, flat panel TVs, and other improvements. They even included a humble but nice breakfast every morning at no extra charge. Super 8 was now a refreshingly pleasant experience for an economy hotel chain.

The challenge was that almost no one knew it. All the data we pored through—quantitative, qualitative, demographic, behavioral, psychographic—signaled that the audience didn't know how elevated the hotel experience had become. The brand had a great story to tell.

The brand wanted to grow by winning over a younger crowd, who were even less likely than older groups to respond to interruptive television ads. It wouldn't be enough to only show potential customers the new rooms in a 30-second commercial or banner ad and offer a discount. Super 8 wanted to celebrate the spirit of the great American road trip to make an emotional connection with the audience.

Soon after we kicked off our collaboration with Super 8, I spoke at a marketing conference where a presenter talked about telling an entire brand story in six seconds. The reason was that YouTube gives viewers the option to skip most ads after the first six seconds. Part of me was impressed that the industry was finally confronting the fact that consumers no longer tolerate interruptions. But I was mostly angry: *Can't we do something better than cram an entire story into six seconds?*

Our team recommended a strategy we call full-funnel brand storytelling that would get past the audience's cognitive spam filters. We would help the brand celebrate people doing interesting things on the road and depict the brand as a refuge for travelers. It was sparked by the simple concept of creating a "Super 8 Film." The title played off one of the original film formats used by Steven Spielberg and other titans of the movie industry.

Our creative team searched for authentic protagonists for these films. We considered a teenage champion rock climber who travels the country with her mom while competing in events, and a young rock star who is fighting a life-threatening illness while touring clubs and singing about the meaning of life. All were interesting but not perfectly aligned with the spirit of the brand. Then we found something amazing in the sea of data about Super 8. We found one data point that was wildly positive. It would change everything.

The owner of a Super 8 franchise in Michigan put up a simple sign next to his best parking spot: "Veteran Parking, Reserved Because You Served." He saved the best spot in his lot exclusively for veterans. On social media, people were talking about how much they loved this hotel and the owner's simple gesture. It was a classic example of audience empowerment turning to brand evangelism.

Digging deeper, we realized that Super 8 had a great heritage of supporting veterans, including successful promotions every Veterans Day. This wasn't simply a data point; it was an insight about Super 8's target audience that eventually led us to Ian, Gino, and the Human Hug Project.

Full-Funnel Storytelling Solves an Old Problem with New Technology

Though some pundits think the sales funnel is an outdated concept, it remains the clearest way to think about how customers are acquired. At the top, which is the largest section, is awareness of a brand. In the middle of the funnel, where it gets narrower, are interest and consideration. At the bottom of the funnel, the narrowest section, is purchase and evangelism. The classic funnel is elegant in its simple depiction of the customer journey.

Historically, brands concentrated on the top and bottom of the funnel. They used mass media (largely TV, radio, and print ads) to build awareness. Then, in the lower funnel, they used conversion techniques such as coupons and direct mail promotions. The problem with this approach was that the two phases weren't connected. A brand might buy a lot of TV in a region, which would make people there much more aware of it. Later, a different team at the company would send direct mail to the same zip codes, hoping that it would reach people who were already primed by seeing the TV ads.

But there was no sure way for brands to know if those who got the direct mail had seen the TV ad. This resulted in a large amount of waste and inefficiency. More importantly, it left out the most important part of the story: what makes a brand different and better. The middle of the funnel is where consumers spend most of their time assessing the values, features, and functionality of products. Yet most brands still overinvest in the top and/or bottom of the funnel. The former often leads to awareness without sales, while the latter often leads to a costly addiction to discounts and promotions that damage brand affinity.

A full-funnel storytelling strategy solves these problems. Rather than spending heavily to drive awareness at the top and then jumping to promotions at the bottom, we can connect all of the touchpoints in between. This is probably the most exciting breakthrough enabled by digital marketing. Digital tools like sequential messaging, custom audiences, and content retargeting can finally connect the entire funnel, allowing us to tell a compelling story across the customer journey.

Full-funnel storytelling enables a brand to personalize its message based on an individual's behavior, psychographics, and, most importantly, previous interactions with the brand. Nobody wants to be treated generically. Nobody wants to hear the same ad over and over again.

Use the Top of the Funnel to Drive Awareness with Emotional Storytelling

Super 8 positions itself as the ultimate road trip companion and wanted to support the Human Hug Project's efforts with a full-funnel story, so we reached out to Ian and Gino, offering them travel assistance and free hotel stays. The chain also paid for a camera crew to help document the Human Hug Project, promote it online, and help them raise money.

Over the course of an entire month, we traveled with them to veterans hospitals, filming the hugs and human connections. The first time I met Gino, we sat alone in a room with two cameras and a bank of lights. Thick cables streamed out of the gear and under a door to the next room, where a team was watching and listening to the interviews on monitors.

Gino told me the story of a Vietnam veteran who had been exposed to Agent Orange and struggled with PTSD for decades. He was fighting cancer. His daughter was in the room. She didn't understand why her father was always so angry and thought he hated her. When Ian and Gino arrived, this tough Vietnam veteran reluctantly accepted a hug and then broke down in tears as 40 years of hate and anger melted. Through the tears he apologized to his daughter for the years of mistreatment. Compassion started to conquer anger. Gino and I both cried while he shared the story.

Instead of making a 30-second TV spot or a six-second YouTube pre-roll, we turned the best footage into a six-minute mini-documentary, supplemented by shorter videos, still photos, and write-ups. Perhaps our most important decision was not to focus on Super 8 in the story. If you look carefully, you can see a Super 8 hotel in the background of the videos for a few seconds. But the focus is truly on Ian, Gino, and their authentic mission to help their fellow veterans. Plugging the clean new rooms at Super 8 would have ruined the emotional storytelling at the top of the funnel, when our goal was merely to raise awareness and position the brand. Viewers could see that Super 8 was the sponsor, and that was enough for now.

Our mini-documentary about the Human Hug Project went viral. Millions watched, shared, and commented on the video. On social media, the conversation around Super 8 fundamentally changed. People were talking about how proud they were of Super 8 for doing something so important for veterans. The hotels soon benefited from their association with the Human Hug Project, with positive comments about the experience of staying there streaming through their social channels.

Without relying on TV ads and the egregious expense of creating and placing those ads, we changed the perceptions of the Super 8 brand at the top of the funnel. The next step was to convert all that goodwill into bottom-line results by improving Super 8's numbers of "heads in beds." We didn't simply tell the story of the Human Hug Project; we made it the first phase of a full-funnel campaign.

Use the Middle of the Funnel to Build Interest with Functional Content

Even in the age of short attention spans, people spend a lot of time in the funnel. Before booking a vacation, for instance, the average person now visits 38 websites over the course of 10 to 20 hours, and even more for an unfamiliar destination. Most of that time is spent mid-funnel, which I think of as a digital playground. Instead of being constrained by 30-second ads to show the functional reasons why a person might want a product, brands can use any creative or technological format that they want.

In the middle of the funnel, people are dreaming and researching across a variety of sources including retail stores, websites, review platforms, and conversations with friends and family. Some spend hours engaging with videos on social media and YouTube. This makes the middle the most exciting place in modern marketing. It's where revolutionary change is truly possible.

Before the internet took off, brands didn't really have tools for the middle of the funnel. They had to rely on retail stores for effective merchandising, and they had to trust salespeople to communicate features and benefits. But now brands can leverage all of their creativity, technology, data, and analytics to create meaningful content that people want to absorb, rather than skipping past as fast as humanly possible. The only limitation is our imagination.

When we think about exponential brands that successfully differentiate themselves—Fender providing interactive lessons to help new guitarists, Patagonia creating documentaries that defend the environment, 805 Beer filming videos that entertain outdoor enthusiasts—these are primarily mid-funnel initiatives. They help the audience understand what makes a brand different and better than the competition, and what values it stands for.

For the Human Hug Project, we followed up on the mini-documentary by reaching out to people on social media who interacted with our content, since they were already emotionally engaged. We used a series of posts and other content to explain that the proud sponsor of the Human Hug Project was also the place to find clean, stylish, beautiful rooms across the country. Data showed us that the best way to put a head in a bed was to show the rooms. Functional information may seem boring, but in the mid-funnel it empowers people. Through interactive video and images, we showed how appealing those rooms were and how much value for your travel dollar you could now get at a Super 8. These messages served as the transition path between awareness and purchase.

Use the Bottom of the Funnel to Close the Sale with Calls to Action

To recap: at the top of the funnel, we partnered with the Human Hug Project to show our target audience that Super 8 values and supports veterans. In the middle of the funnel we shared functional, empowering information about the experience people would have at the hotels. Finally, for the conversion phase, we used geotargeting to offer discounts and promotions to travelers who had already seen the upper and mid-funnel content, were near a Super 8, and whose clicks around the web showed that they were planning a trip.

We were able to do this by rethinking how direct response advertising is developed. For decades, various kinds of promotional offers have flooded our mailboxes, interrupted our dinners with telemarketing cold calls, and filled our newspapers and magazines. About 20 years ago, someone figured out that brands could track and "retarget" consumers based on their online behavior. We all remember that first moment when we were shopping for a pair of shoes, and the next moment that same pair of shoes followed us around in banner ads across the web. Some of us found it a little creepy at first, but we now recognize it's largely unthreatening and even valuable to us. It makes advertising slightly less annoying because the messages highlight products that we are interested in.

Now, rather than relying on somebody to look at a product and then following up with an ad about it, we're able to use the same technology to deliver a piece of content and then follow it up with another piece of content to tell a full brand story. If people interact with that content, we can follow up with another and another, and so on until they convert. We are shifting from product retargeting to sequential content delivery that leads the audience in a process from becoming aware and interested to converted and evangelizing.

Marketing messages at each phase of the funnel can have an impact in isolation, but they are far more valuable when combined in an optimal sequence. Research shows that information is remembered 40 percent more effectively if told in the correct sequence.

Because we offered discounts and promotions only to people who were already emotionally engaged and were strong prospects, the results were incredible. While a typical lower-funnel promotional campaign might generate $2 in revenue for every $1 spent on marketing, and a good campaign might pay off 3x, the ROI for Super 8 was *13x*. That's a lot of heads in beds.

Leveraging the Entire Purchase Journey Builds Psychological Momentum

It's not enough to create content for each stage of the funnel. Brands need to rotate the funnel sideways and look at each step of the modern purchase journey, which has dozens of points where brands and consumers interact.

Historically, brands could get by with one big and clever ad campaign. Today, they need to create experiences and smaller pieces of content that address granular needs at each step of the purchase journey. Delivering the right kind of messages at each point in the funnel generates psychological momentum, the concept we explored when discussing Apple's retail stores. Momentum steadily moves people through their journey by building their confidence in a brand and removing sources of friction. It's incredibly powerful because brands can now create snackable forms of content on social and digital media to steadily move each person along their unique journey. To get a sense of how this works, look at the following paragraph:

> As you read this paragraph, your brain _____ in the blanks so you _____ read it easily, even _____ you can't see every word. Our brains simply fill _____ the blanks, so you _____ easily comprehend it.

This is very similar to strong modern brand storytelling. While it's nearly impossible for a brand to master every touchpoint perfectly, and while the audience may skip over some of them, they can still complete their journeys in a coherent and meaningful way. Unfortunately, most brands address their customers more like this:

> As you read this paragraph, I made you laugh and cry, so when you're in the market for _____ and you really need _____ in the _____ so _____ you _____ _____ it _____, even _____ you can't _____ every _____. Our _____ simply _____ in the _____, so _____ you _____ easily _____ it.

This kind of messaging starts with a strong point but soon loses the thread of communication. From step to step there are too many blanks, which ultimately crushes psychological momentum by creating friction. Both the brand and the audience are deterred from achieving their goals. If you rely exclusively on traditional advertising, you will leave too many blanks.

Most brands these days are decent, if not great, at emotional messaging. The advertising industry has built an entire ecosystem of awards, magazines, blogs, videos, and a seaside city in France that turns itself over to award the year's funniest and most touching ads every year. But that's just for the top of the funnel. You can capture lots of attention and interest with emotional messaging, but you can't drive business results without equal attention to chronological functional messaging.

Brands miss this point when they focus on the macro metrics of how dollars have historically been spent, including the hundreds of billions spent on TV advertising. The problem is that many of those ads are for impulse purchases and undifferentiated products. Most brands are more differentiated than the big-spending megabrands and have a more complex sales cycle. Booking a hotel reservation, for example, is a much more involved process than making a choice about chewing gum or frozen food.

I respect the hell out of the massive companies that can get me to try a new product at the supermarket because I remember a clever ad, but that's a terrible template for the vast majority of brands. Unless you have the massive budgets of a Progressive or Taco Bell, brands will be far better off creating meaningful content for the entire journey rather than interrupting people with superficial messages at only a few junctures.

Make the Customer the Hero

Storytelling is as much a science as it is an art. You've probably heard of the Hero's Journey, the plot template popularized by Joseph Campbell that's been used in nearly every major film from *The Godfather* to *Star Wars* to *Braveheart*. A hero goes on an adventure, confronts a crisis, and returns home transformed. After a lifetime of absorbing stories in this basic format, we automatically gravitate toward any sequential narrative that captures and maintains our attention. It's no wonder that people loved the story of Ian, Gino, and the other veterans they met during the Human Hug Project. Their transformations were so emotionally engaging that once the audience started watching the mini-documentary, they had to find out how it ends.

But effective brand storytelling goes further than that—it's ultimately about making the customer the protagonist of his or her own story. We all want to be the hero, but not necessarily in a big, grandiose, emotional way. We don't have to save the world or win a gold medal. We can feel like heroes for something as simple as cooking a great meal for our families, learning to use a new piece of technology, buying the right pair of glasses, learning to play guitar, adding a few pounds of muscle, redecorating the house, throwing a great party, or planning an awesome road trip.

The Super 8 campaign was ultimately about helping guests create their own story by celebrating the spirit of the road. Of course, Ian and Gino were heroes in the traditional sense. But that was only a portion of the overall campaign. By following up their story with functional content about the rooms and then subsequently offering discounts and promotions, we were able to empower the audience. We helped them become the hero of their own journey. For both the veterans and the brand, the results were profound.

Three Exponential Takeaways

- Most brands either overspend at the top of the sales funnel to build awareness or overspend at the bottom of the funnel to acquire customers, but exponential brands are built in the middle of the funnel with content that empowers and differentiates.

- Brands can capture attention with emotional messaging, but they can't drive business results without equal attention to functional messaging.

- Digital tools like sequential messaging, custom audiences, and content retargeting enable brands to tell a compelling story across the customer journey.

And One Question to Ponder

Are you *really* investing in empowering content for the entire consumer journey, or are you overspending on frivolous messages that can easily be ignored?

Transparency means
that modern advertising
simply puts a creative
lens on brand culture.

6 The Why and How of Culture

At the end of one of the most dramatic time periods in business history, Kurt Eichenwald set out on an assignment for *Vanity Fair* to examine what he would eventually describe as Microsoft's Lost Decade. He was investigating a company that had once been the world's largest and most successful, but whose growth had hit a brick wall.

Apple, a company that had been largely irrelevant 10 years earlier, was now the leader in the music, mobile, and tablet categories, even though Microsoft had entered each of them earlier. Google had come out of nowhere to dominate search. Amazon had stepped up to own e-commerce. Microsoft was even losing ground in its bread-and-butter category of operating systems. Kurt arrived on the scene with a simple question: What happened?

A countless number of factors could have led to Microsoft's struggles—hardware, software, international licensing, local governments, piracy, and so on—but every single person he talked to, all 150 of them, pointed to the same reason without being prompted. It all came down to a compensation plan that had destroyed their corporate culture.

I've read countless articles over the past few decades, but no analysis has stuck out the way that Eichenwald's article did. How could it be possible that every single person could give the same response to such a broad, open-ended question?

I grew up with Microsoft. Without it, my entire education would have been different. My entire career would be different. In fact, the entire advertising revolution probably would not have happened without Microsoft. I was dumbfounded by the simplicity of the problem.

Everybody who participated in Eichenwald's interviews cited a system that was originally designed as an incentive but backfired spectacularly. It was called "stack ranking." Essentially, it graded every team member on a bell curve. One set of employees ranked as top performers, another as good performers, and continued down to poor performers. Those who received strong ratings would receive better financial compensation and career advancement. Those who didn't could expect professional stagnation and an eventual exit from the company.

On paper, this sounds like a good idea. Everyone should strive to be a top performer. The problem was that if everyone knows that only a certain percentage of the team will reach that status, incentives become skewed. People no longer have any reason to work together or build synergies with other teams. They simply need to do better than the other people on their own team. Not surprisingly, no one at Microsoft wanted to work with talented team members, because that would diminish their own likelihood of receiving a top grade. They no longer focused on reaching goals, because they had no reason to do so. Instead, they shifted from trying to do great work to making sure their colleagues did not.

In addition to creating friction within each team, the compensation plan also strengthened the silos between teams. In a world where the lines between products, services, software, hardware, commerce, advertising, and customer service are getting blurred, silos kill. While other companies were trying to break down their silos, Microsoft unintentionally made the problem worse. The most talented people in the world had once wanted to work at Microsoft, but not after the silos turned to infighting over seemingly trivial matters. Negative energy was pervasive. All of this came from one small decision that seemed logical at the time.

With stack ranking strangling the culture, Microsoft's stock price flatlined. Its market cap fell by half from a best-in-the-world peak of $510 billion. Meanwhile, Apple, Amazon, and Google skyrocketed in value to become three of the world's most valuable companies.

Microsoft not only had the products and audience to dominate the world, it also had access to the world's greatest advertising agencies and brand storytellers. But it learned the hard way that even modest mistakes in culture can devastate an organization. The math is inescapable: Negative numbers lead to compounded negative results. Top talent leaves the building. Second-rate talent fills in. Resources get misallocated. Profits tank, followed by the stock price. Great advertising can't offset weak culture.

Microsoft eventually brought in new top executives, changed its culture, removed silos, and returned to glory. But many other brands don't survive long enough to turn things around: Blockbuster went bankrupt because its culture was too rigid to fight the disruptions caused by Netflix. Kodak had cutting-edge patents for digital photography and could have become both Instagram *and* Shutterfly, but it went bankrupt because its culture couldn't handle the transition away from film and printed photographs. Sears tried to launch new digital services and e-commerce sites, but it divided its business into 30 different divisions (tires, appliances, clothing, and so on) that created silos just as its archrival Target blended bricks with clicks to create a successful multichannel business model.

Culture can create great companies or destroy them. If you can't get it right, nothing else in this book will matter very much.

Modern Advertising Simply Puts a Creative Lens on Brand Culture

The most glaring reason why culture is so important is that every employee at a company is now a publishing platform.

Employees have the ability to document and share evidence of bad behavior. The classic example is American Apparel, the company that made domestically produced clothing cool again. At its peak, it had more than 250 stores and reported annual revenue of more than $600 million. The brand was growing exponentially and became a household name known for sexy advertisements. But its CEO, Dov Charney, reportedly took the sex appeal way too far and was ousted for sexual misconduct allegations. The audience turned on the brand, and the company filed for Chapter 11 bankruptcy. The company's culture defined the brand more than the product or the advertising did.

More prevalent than brands being punished for bad culture is the fact that culture manifests itself in modern advertising platforms. The music industry provides a perfect example. Fender and Gibson have been two of the most important guitar brands for decades. Virtually every great guitar player, including Jimmy Page, Eric Clapton, Jimi Hendrix, Duane Allman, Angus Young, Bonnie Raitt, and hundreds more played either or both brands.

As technology emerged and opened opportunities for both product development and advertising, the brands took different paths to offset the slowing interest in electric guitars. Fender invested in Fender Play, the platform mentioned earlier that empowers players to learn how to play with an instructional series customized to each student's needs. Individual players can choose their instrument, preferred style, and level. Then the system tracks each student's progress and provides incrementally more challenging lessons. The platform helps grow the category, grow the Fender brand, provide data for targeted advertising, and drive revenue through subscriptions. It's a classic example of redefining advertising to be about immersive, empowering experiences.

Around the same time that Fender Play launched, Gibson went in a different direction. In a classic example of being married to interruptions and superficial messages, it sponsored a TV show called *The Pitch*, where advertising agencies vie to create TV ads for the sponsoring brands. It also decided to launch a lifestyle brand by adorning an expanding array of clothing items with the Gibson logo and then invested in new automated tuning technology for its guitars.

The Pitch was a failure because the agencies attempted to use untargeted interruptions rather than empowering content. The problem with the lifestyle clothing was that it damaged the brand's authenticity by attempting to shift from a niche brand to mainstream. The automated tuning technology was a complete disaster that burned through money because guitarists didn't want a piece of technology on the headstock of their guitars.

In contrast to Gibson, Fender first nailed its brand purpose, then built a team that created an empowering, authentic platform. Unlike traditional advertising campaigns that have a short shelf life, Fender Play has thrived for years with steady improvements to the content and technology. When Covid-19 rocked the planet, forcing people to stay at home, Fender gave away 1 million three-month subscriptions to keep people rocking.

Gibson, unfortunately, filed for Chapter 11 bankruptcy in 2014. Thankfully for guitarists around the world, it has emerged from that process committed to its roots and its culture. Gibson's new leadership has the company focused on the quality of its guitars, largely based on a new listening culture that helped Gibson make improvements to the manufacturing process at its Nashville factory.

Culture Is About Putting People in Position to Do Their Best Work

There are hundreds of books and thousands of articles about corporate culture. A Google search will produce 711 million results in 0.44 seconds. Many of the ideas you'll find are good, but together they can get overwhelming and lead to "paralysis by analysis."

Culture has become such a popular business topic that even my local coffee shop has a sign on the wall with Peter Drucker's famous phrase, "Culture Eats Strategy for Breakfast"—right next to one that says "Coffee Spelled Backwards Is Eeffoc. I Don't Give Eeffoc Until I've Had My Coffee."

Research into culture shows that our obsession is justified. Alex Edmans of the London Business School found that stock market returns for companies in Fortune's "100 Best Companies to Work For" were more than double their peers' over a 28-year period. The Hay Group found that highly engaged employees provide 89 percent greater customer satisfaction and 4x revenue growth compared to disengaged employees. Gallup reports that companies in the top quartile of employee engagement are 22 percent more profitable than those in which everyone is just watching the clock.

With all this information in hand, you'd think that most companies would rush to create great cultures. Yet a survey of 200,000 employees at more than 500 companies found that 71 percent of companies still have mediocre cultures. Making great culture a top priority is easy to say, but hard as hell to do.

Culture isn't a poster on the wall. It's not a set of slogans. It permeates every interaction people have with a brand or company. It's built through people, processes, and tools, requiring compounding inputs to generate powerful, exponential results. It really boils down to one thing: *empowering people to do their best work.*

I had to learn this the hard way, after spending the first decade of our agency completely winging it on culture. I had assumed that a great culture was about creating a fun environment. When our team asked for better culture, I bought more beer, made the stereo louder, and bought all of the cliché toys like foosball and Ping-Pong tables—only to wake up one day to the horrendous sound of Ping-Pong balls echoing through the office, reminding the people who were working hard that others weren't. There's nothing wrong with music and games, but they're not what creates culture.

Culture requires processes to put people in position to do their best work. It comes down to talent acquisition and talent collaboration. Talent acquisition requires priority and process. Talent collaboration requires safety and systems. Let's examine each.

Talent Acquisition Is the Top Priority

Everyone can agree that great organizations and advertisements are built with "A players," but few organizations take the time to define what an "A player" really is and what it means for an organization's unique needs. Defining an A is really easy. We learn about it in middle school. An A is anyone who grades at 95 percent or higher. It is the top 5 percent. When it comes to determining whom you want to hire, you need to figure out if the candidate in front of you is in the top 5 percent of his or her field. It's a simple yet extraordinarily effective equation. At the end of the day, it's a judgment call, and there's no way to know for sure, but at least this provides a tangible target: Out of 20 qualified candidates, is this person the best?

Finding that talent, however, can be a tough task. As a leader, you can't simply say that hiring new candidates is the top priority—you have to allocate the time and resources to reflect this prioritization. In practice, this rarely happens. Every good leader I know has a system for managing her time, energy, and to-do list, but most still never manage to spend enough time recruiting. The higher you rise in an organization, the more demands are placed on your time. Top managers get caught up in the day-to-day pressures of sales, strategy, finance, and operations. Instead of hiring strategically, they wait until a specific need comes up. When a manager is extraordinarily busy, it's hard to find time to tackle anything that isn't immediately pressing. Eventually, the team is short-staffed and needs to hire, but at that point there's no time to apply a rigorous hiring process. It's a classic Catch-22.

The goal is to build a "velvet rope" and have a line of people waiting to get into the organization, much like a line of people waiting to get into a club. Brands need to create content not just for prospective customers but also for prospective employees—content that demonstrates the brand's culture and attracts like-minded new team members. It's critical to ensure leaders consider it a top priority to line up new candidates. It is incredibly hard, but organizational research shows that leaders should plan to spend at least 10 percent of their time meeting and recruiting new team members throughout the year, not just when specific needs arise.

Talent Acquisition Requires a Methodical Process

The advertising industry is filled with people with strong emotional intelligence, but a structured process is absolutely critical for effective recruiting. Without a structured process, it's easy for gut instincts to let us down. I know because I've made some disastrous hiring mistakes over the years.

One time we needed a sales manager and had identified a strong candidate I'll call Dave. He had a stellar résumé and seemed nice. I started the interview with my favorite icebreaker, "What's the best album of all time?"

"The Beatles' *Rubber Soul*," he answered immediately.

I had asked this question hundreds of times before, but Dave was the first candidate who, in my humble opinion, totally nailed it. We made a personal connection and spent most the time talking about music. Small talk isn't a trivial part of the job for a salesperson. I needed to make sure he had sufficient charm and charisma. Dave checked that box easily.

Unfortunately, I didn't have a process to evaluate his technical skills or key personality attributes. Eventually, when we shifted the conversation to salary, I made an offer, and Dave went blank. He appeared to have absolutely no neural activity as he stared right through me. I loved it. The most basic rule of negotiating is that whoever talks first loses. I assumed Dave was a master negotiator. I increased the salary offer by 5 percent, then 10, then 20. At that point, he took it.

A few days later, he started his job. We gave him a desk, a shiny new laptop, and some office supplies. I slid the telephone across his desk and gave him the number of the potential client. Again, Dave's face went completely blank, and there appeared to be no neural activity at all. He stared right through the phone. I, on the other hand, had a pretty massive reaction on my face—all the blood ran right out of it. I realized that I had made a massive mistake. Dave didn't go stone-faced when I met him because he was a gifted negotiator. That was just his reaction whenever he got nervous. I had hired a salesperson who was scared of the telephone.

Like me, many interviewers look to the worst advice that floats around about hiring. It's called the "beer test." When you're interviewing someone, you're supposed to ask yourself, "Is this somebody that I want to have a beer with?" The idea is that if you like the person socially, he or she should be a good fit for the culture of your organization.

This advice is not just misguided, it's dangerous. All it really does is build a homogenous organization. You know who you want to drink a beer with at the end of the day? The person who kicks ass and makes you better at what you do. That doesn't require a "beer test." It requires a methodical process.

Like every successful process, great hiring starts with a brief that ensures everyone is aligned. It then requires a tracking system to track both the candidates' work skills and their fit with the brand's values. Like a creative project kickoff, the entire interviewing team needs to gather to review the brief and the scorecard. Then, it's time to start interviewing.

Elon Musk is reported to have a single question that helps him assess job candidates: "Tell me about some of the most difficult problems you've worked on and how you solved them." This helps identify people who pad their résumés and claim credit for projects on which they had only a cursory role. As he puts it, "The people who really solved the problem know exactly how they solved it. They know and can describe the little details."

The key is to work like a forensic investigator, digging deeper into each clue to understand the underlying components of performance. You have to relentlessly probe why something happened until the candidate reveals her expertise or shortcomings with no ambiguities. Why did this happen? Why did you take the steps you took? Why did you get the results you got?

Asking "why" puts you in an uncomfortable situation. You're speaking to someone who might become a colleague and lifelong friend. Asking why, why, why ultimately feels like you're asking, "What did you do wrong?" Nobody's perfect, and anyone who pretends to be perfect during an interview is raising a different kind of red flag. The question is, how well do they understand and compensate for their flaws? Are they sharing credit with colleagues? Are they taking responsibility for their shortcomings?

Rigorous hiring might force you to miss some great candidates, but it's better to be overly picky for the sake of building a team of absolute A players. A players not only go on to do A work, but they also attract other A players. That creates a positive snowball effect. Success begets success.

Talent Collaboration Starts with Psychological Safety

Like honeybees, humans thrive by maximizing our intelligence through collaboration. Even the earliest humans worked together to bring down much stronger creatures, like woolly mammoths. In modern times, we maximize our collective intelligence to create exponential growth.

Google, which overtook Microsoft during its lost decade, has maniacally studied the power of collaboration, spending millions of dollars measuring and optimizing how its team works together. In 2012, it launched Project Aristotle to study its teams and figure out why some thrived while others stumbled. What it found was highly consistent with what a group of psychologists from Carnegie Mellon, MIT, and Union College learned a few years earlier. Peak performance does not come from raw intelligence, personality, work ethic, or a rigid process. Rather, the largest predictor of team performance comes from psychological safety. It's about ensuring that a team can communicate honestly with each other without unfair repercussions for missteps. It is manifested in small factors that compound for exponential results, such as individuals listening closely and deferring to each other in meetings. It's about treating each other with respect and courtesy.

These are not snowflake points. I'm not suggesting that businesses should insulate people from consequences, but the simple fact is that people function better in an emotionally supportive environment. Positive psychology leads to measurable performance improvements. For example, research shows that if you smile, you run faster. You don't need to have office parties all the time. It's more important to make it clear that taking calculated risks will be appreciated, not punished.

I learned about the power of psychological safety while working as a cook before I entered the advertising industry. Under the hood, the restaurant industry and the ad industry are much the same, blending creativity and commerce. Both industries build teams with disparate skills, rooted in customer service.

A chef named Henrik demonstrated how to lead with psychological safety when I worked for him at a beautiful restaurant in Lake Tahoe. The restaurant served the best food in the area. Henrik would speak in French during intense moments in the kitchen. I had no idea what he was saying when he yelled "Chaud!" while coming down the hall, but it was clear that he wanted everyone to get the hell out of the way. One day Henrik was making a caramel sauce with melted sugar and cream. Caramel is a lot like molten metal; if it touches you, unlike water, it doesn't start cooling off quickly. It holds its temperature and continues to sear right through the skin.

As Henrik came through holding a pot of caramel and yelling "Chaud!" everybody quickly got out of the way—except for one young waitress who froze in his path. They collided and I watched the molten liquid fly through the air. It seemed to pause for a moment midair, like a scene from a Looney Tunes cartoon. A large red-hot blob fell on Henrik's forearm and started to burn through his skin. The edges were bubbling up as his flesh melted. The sound was horrifying, and the waitress next to me covered her mouth and ran out of the room. But Henrik didn't flinch.

The waitress who was responsible for the accident also got a tiny drop of caramel on her wrist. She screamed, and Henrik quickly grabbed a wet towel and wiped her off, leaving barely a red dot, smaller than a mosquito bite. He then took her to the sink and let cool water gently flow over the dot.

He made sure she was completely comfortable—before paying any attention to the melting flesh on his own arm. Meanwhile the molten caramel seeped down to the bone, giving Henrik a significant injury that would leave him bandaged for the entire summer. He never said a single word about it.

Like Henrik, making a team feel safe is the foundation of great culture in the advertising industry. The rate of change is exponential. Using the same techniques as yesteryear is the recipe for failure. Individuals need to think differently. Teams need room to make mistakes. They need to be comfortable admitting and discussing mistakes, then course correcting.

By definition, a revolution means that we don't know what's going to happen next. A team will hopefully get most things right, but people will inevitably make mistakes. Providing a safe, positive environment where intelligent failure is permitted is not merely a humane idea, it's an essential ingredient to success in unsettled times.

Talent Collaboration Requires Customized Systems

Safety is only half of the process for collaboration. Systems are also critically important. Unlike Microsoft during its lost decade, Apple and Amazon worked relentlessly to remove internal barriers so they could focus on the dramatically changing needs of customers. These systems don't get headlines; they're often seemingly small maneuvers that lead to dramatic results.

For instance, when Steve Jobs was building Apple into a behemoth, he would take executive team members from various divisions and bring them together for a multihour Monday meeting. These were some of the brightest, hardest working, and most stressed-out executives on the entire planet, and this was valuable time. There was probably more than a little eye-rolling among them. But Steve would force these meetings to happen using what his biographer, Walter Isaacson, referred to as the "reality distortion field." Among other things, these meetings led to the eventual revolution in retail, which required contributions from finance, operations, technology, retail, marketing, advertising, and probably a bunch of divisions I've never even heard of. It was silo-busting at its finest.

Amazon also owes a good deal of its success to systems that power collaboration. In 2004, for example, Jeff Bezos outlawed the use of PowerPoint presentations. Instead, whoever leads a meeting at Amazon must write a two-to-six-page memo that summarizes the idea. Meetings start with everyone sitting quietly for upwards of 20 minutes to thoroughly read the memo before discussing it in an open setting.

As Bezos explained, "PowerPoint-style presentations somehow give permission to gloss over ideas, flatten out any sense of relative importance, and ignore the interconnectedness of ideas." Instead, he insists on a narrative structure that forces deeper thought and aligned understanding. This approach ensures stronger input from meeting organizers and removes ambiguities for attendees. Starting out in silence may initially feel awkward, but it ensures that everyone is aligned. Even though Amazon is one of the most successful companies in the world, I'm not aware of a single other company that has adopted this practice.

Every organization is unique and needs to find its own approach to the relentless pursuit of collaboration. Today, that requires cloud-based tools and people-based processes to make sure teams are exchanging ideas effectively and efficiently. Organizations need a system to create action items and then record, track, and complete them. Collaboration doesn't happen on its own. It requires a deliberate, documented process.

It's important to recognize that successful collaboration is also about dividing and conquering. Data analysis, brand immersion, and the creative process take time and focus. Recent research shows that two-thirds of senior managers thought meetings kept them from completing their own work, and 71 percent said meetings are unproductive and inefficient. Sixty-four percent said meetings come at the expense of deep thinking, and 62 said meetings miss opportunities to bring the team closer together. Yet the average middle manager spends one-third of her time in meetings, and the average senior manager spends more than half of her time in meetings. Systems help optimize every interaction throughout an organization, including how day-to-day meetings are run.

Culture Is Built through Small Behaviors That Create Cognitive Shortcuts

In a world of transparency, you can detect culture in every interaction. Early on, for example, our agency presented to one of the hottest tech companies in the world. Before the big meeting, I walked around the conference room shaking the hands of the executives and introducing myself with my standard, "Hi, I'm Jeff. Great to meet you."

Suddenly, one of the top execs stopped me. At top volume he yelled, "Last name! When you introduce yourself, say your last name!" We had just met, and he was already yelling at me. As I started presenting, he continued to attack. On the very first slide he was scolding me like I was a kindergartner. I could see the looks of sympathy on the faces of his team members, as if to say, "This is what we deal with every day." I should have walked out mid-presentation, but I was too young for that.

In contrast, when working on the Super 8 brand years later, I had the pleasure of working with Wyndham, a company that treats every guest at its headquarters like a guest at one of its luxury hotels. The first time I was in Wyndham's offices, I asked where I could find the men's bathroom. A man immediately stopped what he was doing and walked me down the hall and around a couple of corners to show me exactly where it was. I didn't know who he was, but given that we were near the offices of C-level executives, he was probably quite senior. Wyndham's culture is all about being helpful and respectful—even with random visitors at the corporate office. This might seem trivial, but it's not. The culture extends to every corner of the organization, and it ultimately flowed into the empathy and collaboration that produced the Human Hug Project for Wyndham's Super 8 brand.

By comparison, the tech company with the yelling executive? It was EarthLink. Once one of the most respected companies in the world, it is now almost nonexistent, having lost 70 percent of its value between 2017 and 2019 alone. You could see both companies' cultures manifested in the smallest behaviors, which created exponential performance, exponentially strong for Wyndham and exponentially devastating for EarthLink.

Culture Is about Team Empowerment

As we've discussed, brands were once free to portray whatever image they wanted. But now customers can see right through fake messaging to understand the values of a company and the quality of its products. Modern advertising simply puts a creative lens on a brand's internal culture. Apple's ads demonstrate a culture rooted in making technology user-friendly. Fender Play demonstrates a culture rooted in a passion for music. Wyndham demonstrates a culture rooted in the love of hospitality.

But culture isn't an obscure concept where advertising teams struggle to make their teams have more fun.

Great culture is simply about putting people in a position to do their best work. Just as brands do their best when they empower their customers, culture works best when it empowers every employee. Those who find themselves in an environment that makes them feel safe, supported, respected, and inspired by the company's values will generate exponential results.

In a world with unprecedented access to data and technology, culture is the true competitive advantage. Technology will continue to evolve at an exponential pace, but humans will always be core to successful advertising. In fact, as brands use technology to play an ever-growing role in the lives of their customers, human insight will only grow in importance. Companies will spend whatever it takes to achieve technical parity. The true differentiators will still be creativity, teamwork, personality, and the synergies created by human beings.

Fortunately, culture is never set in stone, and even the most broken cultures are never beyond redemption. When Satya Nadella became CEO of Microsoft in 2014, a lot of people had written off the company. How could this soft-spoken, well-read, thoughtful engineer possibly turn things around?

One of Nadella's first moves as CEO was to have the company's top executives read Marshall Rosenberg's *Nonviolent Communication*, which focuses on empathy and collaboration. It was a signal about a shift in culture from infighting to teamwork. Nadella spent his first year on the job on a listening tour, absorbing everything he could from his employees. He even went on record saying that creating a culture that listened, learned, and harnessed individual passions and talents was his chief job as CEO. In the first chapter of his book, *Hit Refresh*, where he lays out his core thesis statement, Nadella demonstrates his commitment to culture by using the word *empathy* 22 times, basically the same number of times he used the word *technology*.

Eventually, Nadella replaced stack ranking with an incentive system that rewarded collaboration and cooperation. It facilitated a shift in focus from desktop operating systems and software to the cloud and productivity software. The results speak for themselves. In the seven years since Nadella took the helm, Microsoft has completely turned itself around, growing its market capitalization more than 6x. It has also regained its status as one of the world's top technology companies, competing at the same level as Amazon, Google, and Apple.

Culture isn't touchy-feely. It isn't soft. It isn't esoteric. It isn't a task for the HR department. It's one of the most important tools for driving exponential growth.

Three Exponential Takeaways

- Culture isn't a poster on the wall. It's not a set of slogans. It's built through people, processes, and tools. It really boils down to one thing: empowering people to do their best work.

- Research into culture shows that our obsession is justified. It has a direct impact on profitability.

- There is a methodical process that can be used to build culture. It includes talent acquisition (prioritizing and applying process to recruiting new team members) and talent collaboration (using safety and systems to build synergies).

And One Question to Ponder

Are you using advertising to cover up your brand's culture or to bring it to life?

The best ideas don't always win. You need to get others to believe in them.

7 Selling the Big Idea

I knew the answer to the question before I picked up the phone, but as an agency owner, I had to make the call. My contact at Discovery Channel answered on the third ring. I asked him how we did in the pitch. "Jeff," he said, "I had a million dollars for you. All you had to do was not screw it up."

But we had screwed it up. Completely and utterly. We had great insights. We had great strategy. We had great ideas. We had great creative. It should have been a slam dunk. But we had a terrible presentation.

We weren't uniquely incompetent. In fact, we did exactly what people in our industry do all the time. And we got the same results. Our approach to that pitch remains one of the core issues that is holding the industry back.

I still remember the moment it all went south. Ten of us were sitting around the table, five on our side, five on theirs. We were about 25 minutes in, and everyone was getting bored. Then we put up a slide that consisted of a table with eight columns and six rows. Each cell contained a different data point in a tiny font. For some inexplicable reason, we decided to read the contents of the entire table to them, cell by cell.

We were losing the audience, and I was on high alert. Off to one side, I heard one of the executives lean over to a colleague and whisper in her ear, "This is a genius presentation." She didn't say it because we were geniuses. She was being facetious. We were trying to *prove* that we were geniuses but were being painfully boring instead. There was no energy. No intrigue. No enthusiasm. No momentum. And no chance.

After spending a full 25 minutes on the data-stuffed slide, we presented a beautiful campaign full of digital, video, and social activations for the brand. It was a breakthrough idea with empowering content that would have led the target audience through the sales funnel. I still believe it could have been a game-changer for Discovery Channel. But by the time we got to the good stuff, we had already sucked all of the excitement out of the room and all of the glucose out of their brains. They were all just saying to themselves, *"Please get the hell out of our conference room."* Discovery, sadly but deservedly, is not a client of ours.

The Great Irony: An Industry That Influences Millions Stinks at Internal Influence

It's our responsibility as marketers to get brands to make changes that keep up with the exponential changes taking place in consumer behavior. It's our responsibility to inspire bold action. But the great irony is that while advertisers are trained to influence people in the marketplace, we tend to be horrible at influencing each other internally.

Great sales skills are absolutely critical for driving exponential results. Not just selling products to consumers but, perhaps more importantly, selling ideas to internal teams. If you can't get your own people excited about a brand's vision, strategy, tactics, culture, and processes, not much else will matter.

Our experience at Discovery Channel is fairly commonplace. Every day, around the world, hundreds of similarly brain-dead presentations attempt to beat people over the head with logic until they submit. Somehow, we have come to believe that with enough data, we can eliminate risk. We've become addicted to information overload. We may have breakthrough ideas, but they get left on the cutting room floor because we present them so poorly.

When it comes to consumer-facing stories, brands over-index on novelty and emotion. In today's advertising, you can find plenty of moms, dads, dogs, cats, polar bears, and people doing impossibly cute things or overcoming incredible odds. But among ourselves in conference rooms, where everyone is trying to climb the corporate ladder, no one wants to make a mistake. So we go in the opposite direction. We endlessly analyze, strategize, and hypothesize. We create PowerPoint decks filled with data and statistics. We talk about bold thinking but then bore each other to death with dreary communications that fail to inspire our own organizations, which makes it impossible for our ideas to come to life and actually make a difference in the world.

We should never forget that the executives who make big decisions are human beings who are subject to the same pressures, distractions, and information overload as everyone else, if not more so. Like everybody else in the country, 80 percent use their phones first thing in the morning, 62 percent admit to sleeping with their phones, and 88 percent use them in the bathroom. They consume more than 13 hours of media every day. As a result, before most executives even get into a meeting to discuss new ideas, they've been oversold and underwhelmed. They're distracted, resistant, defensive, and bored.

Perhaps the biggest barrier to success is that we have stopped telling stories. Stories, we assume, are frivolous. They don't belong in a serious business context. But humans don't simply love stories. We need stories. We are genetically wired for stories. Since the dawn of early man, we've used stories to transfer information. They are, in fact, what separates us from other creatures on the planet.

Business stories aren't simply about emotionally engaging with a tale that starts with a derivation of "It was a dark and stormy night." The most successful business stories are more about what you don't say rather than what you do. They're about relentlessly stripping away distracting noise to create useful signals. They pare down extraneous information and get to the point as quickly as possible. This doesn't take special genetic skills or massive levels of self-confidence. Rather, it requires a chronological process that methodically engages listeners and moves them along their decision-making journey.

Leveraging Intentional Sales to Drive Decision-Making

There are literally tens of thousands of books and articles on selling. They range from old-school ideas like *Always Be Closing* to the more modern *Art of the Consultative Sale*. I'm not a professional salesperson, but I've bought and sold hundreds of millions of dollars in media and professional services. I've succeeded and flopped. I've watched others do the same. I've learned what works and what doesn't.

It's certainly not about being an aggressive salesperson with a slick pitch and guns blazing. It's about a collaborative process that methodically gets team members aligned. I call it Intentional Sales. It treats the process for selling big ideas the same way any creative project is treated, using a strategy, a team, alignment, and collaboration.

While every team should build out an approach that matches their personality, I've identified four key steps that move the process forward. They include Starting at the Finish Line, which defines and sets goals for each interaction; the Listening Tour, which puts a mathematical emphasis on listening more than talking; the Inverted Triangle, which engages the audience with big ideas instead of granular details; and Managing the Outcome, which ensures that every interaction moves the process along a path with a clearly defined action item. Let's dig in.

Start the Sales Process at the Finish Line

The first step in Intentional Sales is to Start at the Finish Line by defining the exact environment and desired outcomes for every interaction. I'm not just talking about presentations and other big moments. It's the lunchtime meeting, the quick huddle around the laptop, the one-on-one with your boss, the summary email. Very rarely in today's complex business environment is one person responsible for selling a big idea. It's almost always a team. Starting at the Finish Line means getting everyone on the team to fully understand the exact environment in which your story will be told and the minimum acceptable goal for each step of the process.

The environment is something people rarely think about, but without defining it, it's almost impossible to nail the granular elements needed to fight friction and generate success. Are you emailing a story with an attachment? If so, then you can use lots of text. Are you giving the presentation in person? If so, go easy on the text, because it is cognitively impossible to listen thoughtfully and read a data table at the same time. Are there eight people in the room or 80? Large groups usually require more high-level emotional story-telling, while small groups might transition more quickly to functional planning. I'm shocked and baffled by how many presentations miss these basic fundamentals. From conference rooms to conference stages, I watch gifted people crush great ideas with information overload.

With the environment fully understood, the next component is to define the ideal outcome from each interaction. Rarely, if ever, is the immediate goal to get somebody to buy an idea or concept. Revolutionary ideas are complex, and the process of introducing them requires multiple meetings, sometimes with dozens of decision makers and influencers. For each interaction, the goal is typically one small, humble step forward: Get the next meeting, get access to additional data, get a brief, get an RFP, or get past the gatekeeper. By defining the goal of the interaction, we can march toward our intended outcome.

As an outsider to the advertising industry, I learned this process the hard way. Before we worked with Suzuki to launch the Busa Beats campaign described earlier, we first needed to get them as a client. Whenever I called to meet their head of marketing, he was willing to invest a few minutes with me. It was a small investment of time for him, but each trip took me a full day of travel and expenses I could barely afford. We would meet in his conference room and pontificate about the future of marketing. We learned about each other's perspectives, but it never progressed from a business standpoint. This went on for about a year, with me slowly bleeding our young agency's limited resources. I never defined success for each meeting, so I never made progress.

After almost going broke, I finally shifted to Start at the Finish Line. I defined the goal for each meeting. Rather than simply pontificate, I used each meeting to understand his specific unmet needs and ended by ensuring we had one small subsequent step planned. I worked with Jordan to design a simple interface for a new website to show our design skills and our ability to address his functional needs. After gaining a small win with those mock-ups, we built out interactivity and added surrounding slides with insights and action items. It took us months to complete the process, but once we Started at the Finish Line, we were able to manage small steps that generated big results. We eventually won the account and have done some groundbreaking work together over the past decade.

Collaboration Is Fueled by a Listening Tour

The process for selling a big idea starts with a Listening Tour, which is based on strategic conversations with key stakeholders, who can be anyone from customers and junior employees to customer service reps and top-level executives. These discussions should never be casually explorative. We keep a database of questions and spend hours before big meetings collectively strategizing on which questions should be asked and how they should be customized. The goal is to uncover and understand the unmet, unanswered, and even unknown needs of the audience.

This may seem simple, but the hardest part of listening is not talking. We've all seen vendors who insist on blabbing on and on about what their technology does, how great their media is, or, God forbid, the background and history of their organization. Nobody cares about the backstory or how the founders met in college; people care about having their problems solved.

So, how much should you listen compared to how much you talk? I've learned over time to rely on nature. Mathematically, there's something known as the *golden ratio*. It can be seen in ferns, sunflowers, pinecones, hurricanes, and even the huge spiral galaxies in space. Artists, architects, and others have used the golden ratio extensively. You can see it in Leonardo da Vinci's *Mona Lisa*, Salvador Dalí's *Sacrament of the Last Supper*, even the great pyramids of Egypt and the Pantheon in Athens. Modern designers use it to find the proportion of headlines to body copy or apply it to logo design, most notably Pepsi's.

The golden ratio is created by the Fibonacci sequence, which is constructed by starting with zero and one and then calculating a series of numbers in which each number is the sum of the previous two numbers. It goes: 0, 1, 1, 2, 3, 5, 8, 13, 21, and so on. As the Fibonacci sequence increases in value, the relationship of the numbers converges on the golden ratio of 62 to 38. It suggests that you should listen about 62 percent of the time and talk only about 38 percent.

That proportion provides plenty of time to absorb information while giving space to ask questions and establish a connection with the audience. It might seem like a cheap mnemonic device, but selling big ideas can get stressful, and it's helpful to have a tool to remind oneself that there is, in fact, a natural target that ensures that we focus on listening more than talking.

The crash and burn we had with Discovery Channel was far from my first disaster in a corporate conference room. I learned about the importance of listening more than talking the hard way at a time when we couldn't afford hard lessons. After the dot-com implosion that put every one of our clients out of business forced us to find projects with established brands, our director of business development, Todd, landed a pitch meeting with The Gap, which was then at the peak of its popularity.

We were pitching for a project that would seem small now, but at the time was a game-changing opportunity. Our meeting with two young managers from The Gap, about the same age as Todd and me, started out great. About 15 minutes into it, they basically bought the project. We shifted into personal conversations and quickly started to become friends. Todd made plans to hang out with them over the weekend.

Unfortunately, that's when I kicked the sales pitch into high gear. I shifted the friendly conversation back to business and kept selling them on how great we were, the quality of our data analysis, the creativity of our content, our unparalleled customer service. For a moment, I thought I was doing my best work. But then I saw their faces and body language shift from wanting to be our friends to wanting no part of us. By blathering on and on, I made us look less and less appealing. I tried to sell what was already sold. I positioned us as a company less interested in fully understanding our clients' needs and more interested in touting our own expertise.

We didn't get the gig after all. Todd was livid. He took me outside of their office, grabbed me by the shoulder, and taught me one of the most important lessons of my career: "Shut the hell up." It cost me a big opportunity and a week of lost sleep, but it was worth it. Managing the golden ratio would have saved me the pain.

Great Presentations Leverage the Inverted Triangle

While listening is critical in early stages of the process, eventually it's time to present ideas. Whether it's done over the phone, in an office, in a conference room, or in a ballroom, the most successful presentations are structured like an Inverted Triangle. They start broad with the big idea, and then taper down into more granular elements.

Unfortunately, people often do the exact opposite, starting with granular details and then building to a powerful conclusion. Most presentations fail from the first slide because they start with an agenda slide. If you have a few key points to share upfront, that's fine, but when you're reading seven agenda bullet points, it basically says to the audience, "Here's the same old mind-numbing presentation that you've seen a million times before." Then, presentations often continue the debacle with data summaries and methodological overviews, attempting to demonstrate how much hard work went into the development of a big idea.

People work in advertising specifically because it's cool and creative. There are certainly more lucrative industries. It's critical to understand this mindset and ensure that presentations are engaging before they get granular. And it's not just about engagement, it's also about cognitive shortcuts. Boring presentations send a signal that the actual advertising execution is likely to be boring, ultimately leading to wasted dollars.

Every biological system is also an economic system. Our brains have limited resources that they seek to deploy efficiently to help us survive and thrive. They take up only around 2 percent of our weight but burn 20 percent of our oxygen and glucose. Bad presentations deplete the brain's fuel source, literally choking a person out like a UFC fighter.

Successful influence is about getting people to use as little energy as possible to understand as much as possible. Human brains operate like a sequential processors and are only able to manage one piece of information at a time. In order to understand a person speaking to you, you need to process 60 bits of information per second. In general, humans have a processing limit of 120 bits per second, so it is barely even possible to understand two people talking to you at the same time.

The same is true when someone talks over a complex slide. There's just too much cognitive fuel required. People can't listen to the speaker and read the slide at the same time. That was the mistake we made with Discovery Channel. We drowned our audience with excessive details before we gave them a reason to care. We showed them an appendix, not a presentation.

In my experience, a great presentation is less about hitting the high points than about avoiding the low points, because that's where you lose your audience. That's when they look away, turn on their phones, and stop listening. One wasted bullet point, one wasted moment, one wasted slide, and the audience will become distracted. Everybody is suffering from some kind of digitally-driven attention deficit disorder.

Your competition is the supercomputer sitting in everyone's hand. Once people in the audience look at their phones, it's game over. There's almost no way to fully pull their attention back from the infinite distractions and stress embodied in an executive's smartphone.

Neurologically speaking, the secret to effective internal communications is exactly the same as we have seen with consumers. We need to gain access to the prefrontal cortex. As advertisers, we do this all the time by using novelty and emotion, but we abandon those strategies in a business environment. Instead, we fall back on facts, figures, and data points that simply don't make an impact. Of course, facts and figures are critical, but delivering them up front without any emotional priming overwhelms and bores the audience.

People are already flooded with data points, facts, and figures. It's shockingly hard to share a data point that executives don't already know given that they've dedicated their careers to the brand they are running. They don't need more data. They need insights. They need ideas. They need solutions. Start by capturing attention with novelty, emotion, or big attention-grabbing ideas. Then let the content taper down into more granular topics such as key performance indicators, channel tactics, and production details.

Business storytelling is not the same as dramatic storytelling. In business, you eventually have to introduce granular and boring information as part of explaining complex processes, tools, and data. Once the audience is hooked and has given cognitive permission to leave the emotional realm, people will actually pay attention to data and details. That's how the Inverted Triangle works, first with big, broad ideas and then methodically tapering into more granular details. It first engages and then enables action.

That was the genius of Scott Harrison's presentation to our team about charity: water. He didn't start with an agenda. He didn't start by talking about the compelling evidence that hundreds of millions of people are severely damaged by the absence of clean water. He started by stripping the story down to a key point, using powerful photos that told a story and forced us to pay attention. Nobody even remembered that their phones existed for the hour we spent with him.

Manage the Outcome

Big ideas can be scary. They need to be socialized throughout organizations across multiple calls, emails, meetings, texts, and presentations before they can get approved. Launching a big idea can be a career-defining decision that affects an entire organization. It takes multiple steps, multiple decision layers, and multiple layers of management. It requires alignment on critical strategic issues: Does it fit within the brand's identity? Does it demonstrate the brand's values? Does it authentically fulfill customers' needs? Will it drive key performance indicators? Is the organization structured to successfully launch the idea?

Managing the Outcome is about going into every interaction knowing the ideal result and methodically moving toward that outcome. It brings us full circle back to the first step of Starting at the Finish Line. The ideal outcome might be another meeting. It might be an introduction to a higher-up. It might be a new draft of a concept mock-up. It might be a small pilot project.

Too often in our industry, we have the incredible experience of geeking out on a hot new idea for an hour. When the meeting is over, it feels like we've solved massive challenges, but we don't have a concrete process for the next steps. Time kills all deals. In an age where we are constantly bombarded with data, technology, vendors, ideas, and opportunities, it's easy for executives to lose their enthusiasm about an idea. It's critically important to ensure that each interaction has a defined outcome and timing for the next steps.

This may seem simple and obvious, but in the rush to get day-to-day tasks done it can be uncomfortable to end an email or conversation with specific next steps and timing. It can feel pushy and unnatural, but it's not. It's respectful.

It demonstrates that the time spent was not wasted, and the topic is worthy of additional discussion. Sales processes like Always Be Closing are unpleasant, but Managing the Outcome is not about closing. It's about being respectfully methodical. It's about demonstrating confidence in an idea and managing everybody's time while moving from step to step.

For example, when Scott Harrison came by our agency to talk to us about charity: water, he didn't simply tell us an incredible story and leave. He continued with small steps to help his story spread exponentially: We met in my office and I interviewed him for this book; he introduced us to other team members for pro bono work and invited us to his annual gala. Every one of those outcomes felt not only natural, but empowering. We were emotionally engaged and wanted to continue investing in the relationship. Managing the Outcomes isn't uncomfortable or awkward, it's a natural sequence that simply needs to be part of a methodical process.

Putting It Together: The Human Hug Project

When we worked with Wyndham on the Human Hug Project for its Super 8 brand, we followed this process almost to the letter. Jordan met the CMO by chance on an airplane, and we weren't even sure if the company needed our agency. So we took things incrementally.

In our first meeting with leaders, for example, we didn't offer any ideas or pitch the agency, because we didn't understand their needs. Instead, we simply asked them to give us half an hour so we could learn about their challenges. We asked questions about the hotel, the rooms, the experience, the audience, the metrics, the goals. We wanted to know about the brand story and the overall experience: how guests should feel at the hotel and how prospects should feel when considering the hotel.

Then we briefly emphasized how powerful stories could be for building brands and acquiring data. At one point, Jordan made the offhand comment that we should do something called Super 8 Films. After the meeting, I asked him what he meant by Super 8 Films. He said, "You know, Super 8 Films like Steven Spielberg. All those classic movies were shot on Super 8. Get it?"

Jordan not only has great ideas, but also has the vision to see them as if they are already fully executed. It's a gift, but it's also a challenge. When he makes an offhand comment, he already has the entire idea fully envisioned in his mind. The rest of us do not. He explained the history of film and how we could play off of it by connecting Super 8 hotels to Super 8 Films. We decided to bring it to life, one small step at a time.

We slowly collaborated with the clients to figure out what would work. Rather than build a big pitch deck, we mocked up a few simple storyboards to bring the idea to life. We didn't ask for an hour, just another 15 minutes of their time. We used beautiful imagery, with the main story elements in the foreground and the setting blurred in the background. It was simple Intentional Sales with the goal of building enthusiasm for a potentially powerful idea.

At that point, we didn't have everything solved. We just had the core idea of a story. We showed how data could be used to identify the appropriate protagonists and engage our target audience with an emotional and functional story.

Wyndham was intrigued. The next time we came back, we had a short edit of a video that captured the essence of the idea. Our approach wasn't to solve the entire problem, but rather to move one more step forward so they could envision what the concept might feel like in practice.

Eventually, the Inverted Triangle tapered and we showed some complex slides filled with data, insights, and action items. Wyndham executives are incredibly smart; they wouldn't sign off on a major campaign based on photos and videos. They needed to understand every granular element—but we waited until they were aligned and engaged before going into the data weeds with them.

This process enabled us to incrementally build affinity and raise their comfort levels. If we had burst through the door during our first meeting and told them we had a great idea, it wouldn't have worked. For every action, there is a reaction. We had to move the ball forward slowly and methodically.

Eventually, we got the green light and dove into campaign development, using a process rooted in data, strategy, and collaboration. As we saw earlier, the Human Hug Project attracted millions of viewers and drove conversations that led to profound business results. It all started with a disciplined, intentional approach.

In the Land of the Blind, the One-Eyed Man Is King

Only around one in nine people have a job in sales. The rest of us chose other careers in part because we *didn't* want to sell. But success doesn't simply come from great ideas and great work; it comes from getting a team fully aligned to ensure that those ideas are actually implemented.

I'm surrounded by people who are more talented and skilled than I am. I don't write copy. I don't design. I don't use Photoshop. I can't shoot or edit videos. But I know that many of these incredibly skilled people have never learned to effectively communicate what they believe in. And I know that you can draw a direct line between people's ability to sell their ideas and the arc of their careers.

My father was a salesperson, but my mother, the shrink who spent her career understanding the human psyche, hammered how important it is to sell—even at a very young age when we had those "What do you want to be when you grow up?" conversations. "Jeff, it doesn't matter what you want to be," she would say. "First you need to learn to sell. Whether you want to be a doctor, a lawyer, or a CEO, the greatest leaders are all great salespeople. Not just at selling products, but at selling their ideas." That may have been the single best piece of business advice I've ever been given.

Decades later, Daniel Pink would be considered one of the world's foremost authorities on influence, authoring *To Sell Is Human* along with other bestsellers. In speeches, his core point uses almost the exact same words that my mother used around the dinner table. Unfortunately, most businesspeople were not raised this way. They either never commit to selling or become intimidated by convoluted processes and cheesy advice. Pink has become one of the world's most influential content creators largely based on this simple insight: Selling is human. Watch young children when they want something from their parents, and you realize that people are born knowing how to sell. Somehow, society takes that skill away from us and hampers our ability to launch big ideas.

As the saying goes, "In the land of the blind, the one-eyed man is king." Very few people have the confidence, conviction, or process to sell effectively. Just committing to a process will give you a huge leg up.

Go Ahead and Curse. Or Say Um. Authenticity Is Key.

There are as many different ways to sell as there are people. I'm a loud talker and continue to curse too often, but somehow it works for me. My business partner, Jordan, is much calmer, talks at a lower volume, and tends to say "um" a lot. But he can sell his ideas because he's found his authentic voice. There is no formula.

We still get nervous and awkward like anybody else. We still fail miserably on a regular basis. But our methodical process creates a competitive advantage.

In our Discovery presentation, we missed every one of the recommendations outlined in this chapter. It might appear that our chances were ruined by that overwhelming slide with 48 cells of facts and figures, but we actually started failing much earlier than that. We lost the room at the beginning of the presentation when we showed them a boring agenda followed by some boring facts that they, as top executives, undoubtedly already knew.

Perhaps most importantly, we didn't have a relationship rooted in strong listening and deep understanding. If we had, we would have known what was most important to them and started the presentation there. Or, perhaps because of the time we spent together, one of them would have been comfortable saying, "We have this data already, let's move forward." Without an established relationship or audience engagement, we stood no chance. Our ideas didn't even get considered.

Selling today has nothing to do with the used car salesman of yesteryear. It's an essential skill because the world needs big, bold thinking to move forward. We can have groundbreaking, industry-defining ideas, but if we can't convince anyone to do them, we might as well not have them in the first place. We will be stuck with incremental, not exponential results.

Three Exponential Takeaways

- Selling today has nothing to do with the used car salesman of yesteryear. It's an essential skill because the world needs big, bold thinking to move forward.

- Selling a big idea is the same as any other creative endeavor. It requires a strategy, a team, alignment, and a methodical process.

- Every biological system is also an economic system. Successful influence is about getting people to use as little energy as possible to understand as much as possible. Whoever says the most in the least amount of words wins.

And One Question to Ponder

Think about the last big idea you were passionate about that hit the cutting-room floor. Did you simply try to convince others it was a great idea, or did you use a methodical process to engage and align them?

Brands must prepare
for exponential growth
long before it happens.

8 Prepare to Go Exponential

It was still pitch black out and bitter cold at 5 a.m. in middle-of-nowhere New England. Just a few months earlier, we had been a red-hot agency. Now, we were on the verge of collapse. I was trying to save my company from going out of business. Instead, I was standing in my underwear in a muddy church parking lot with blood dripping off my knuckles.

There was one person on the planet who could save us. He was an investor flying in from China who had just started a holding company that buys hot agencies, which we had been when we met. He had conducted his due diligence and wanted to cut us a check. The agency would be saved, the team would get nice bonuses and career stability. All I had to do was drive to the city, smile warmly, and shake his hand. It was simply a formality, but I was on the brink of disaster.

The problems for our agency happened quickly and deservedly. A few years earlier, we created a documentary called *The Naked Brand*, which introduced the world to the advertising revolution. Its core thesis was that advertising was in the midst of a complete and total revolution. At the first industry conference we went to after its release, I basically told the crowd that everything we had learned over the past 100 years was about to get thrown out and replaced by a completely new model. Many in the audience had spent years at top colleges, grad schools, and corporations, and I told them that their training and education were about to get flushed down the toilet. I didn't know how they would respond. But at the end of the presentation the crowd rose to their feet and gave me a standing ovation. They saw that advertising could be about a lot more than interruptions and superficial messages.

With wind in my sails, I went back to the team for our annual strategic planning meeting. I told them that we wanted to be known as the best agency in the United States. I was succinct. I was clear. I thought I was inspirational. I remember looking out at the people circling me in a series of rows and chairs. About half of them were nodding along, thinking this was a fantastic presentation. I could see them thinking, *"Hell yes, this is exactly what we want."*

But I was also aware that the other half of the agency looked like they were wondering, *"What the hell is this guy talking about?"*

One of them asked, "What does it mean to be the best agency in the United States?"

My answer was, "I don't know, but we'll know it in our hearts when we get there."

The next question was, "What's the timeline to meet this goal?"

My answer was, "I don't know. We'll get there soon."

Jordan, always the pragmatic one, summarized it best as he pulled me aside after the meeting: "You just gave a strategy presentation with no measurable goals, no tangible action items, no process, and no timeline. I'm not sure you're going to get the results you really want."

Jordan's words were prescient, but coming out of that speech we still had enough momentum to become known as the industry's best. We entered a contest for the best agency in the United States. We were tiny compared to most of our competitors, but the judges saw our vision and named us Agency of the Year. The next year, we entered and won again, quickly doubling our agency's size.

Great brands often grow exponentially, moving along at a modest pace for a long time before suddenly and steeply accelerating. When that happens, it feels like a victory, but it's actually quite treacherous. Unfortunately for us, we hit that vertical part of our curve completely unprepared. The phone was ringing off the hook with exciting new projects. Many of them didn't fit our value proposition, but we took them on anyway and lost our focus. We launched projects with inadequate processes, and our quality slipped. We recruited team members without clear criteria, and our culture diminished.

We understood how to use modern advertising to help grow our clients' brands exponentially, but we didn't know that exponential curves required scalable processes for our own company. We weren't prepared for success. Suddenly, we found ourselves hemorrhaging money.

Differentiation Is Being Replaced by Authenticity and Execution

Since the dawn of digital, the number of brands has increased at an exponential rate. Today, more than 500,000 are fighting across the globe for consumers' time, attention, and dollars.

The world has truly become flat. With a few clicks, a kid with a bright idea can find a manufacturing plant in Vietnam, a programmer in Israel, or a logo designer in Brazil. Because of this proliferation of new brands and businesses, there is virtually no white space for forging a unique brand identity. The concept of differentiation is being replaced by authenticity and execution.

The brands I highlighted throughout this book don't offer fundamentally different products or brand identities. What creates value in their brands is the way they authentically bring them to life. Patagonia is ultimately a clothing company that has peers in the marketplace with similar offerings. But when it invests heavily in clothing recycling and immersive content, it is not simply putting on the appearance of a green company—it's educating people and giving them tools to make a difference. Fender makes great guitars, but it's not the only great guitar company out there. When the brand creates a platform to teach people how to play guitar, it's not simply trying to sell—it's helping people fulfill their dreams. When charity: water makes it easy to set up a fundraising campaign, it's not simply trying to raise donations like virtually every other charitable organization—it's helping people make a bigger impact on the world than they can by themselves. It's not the positioning that builds these brands, it's the authenticity and execution.

The importance of successful execution is rooted in psychology. Strong brands benefit from the psychological process of confirmation bias, while weak brands suffer from cognitive dissonance. Confirmation bias is our tendency to absorb information that's consistent with our existing beliefs while filtering out information that contradicts them. When brands emotionally engage us by improving our lives, even in small ways, their products seem more appealing. Customers of Patagonia, Fender, and charity: water spend millions and millions of dollars on them each year because they associate the quality of the products with the beliefs of the companies.

Cognitive dissonance, on the other hand, is the state of having inconsistent and conflicting thoughts that make us feel uncomfortable. When brands say one thing but act in the opposite way, it triggers our anger to the point that we want to punish them with a boycott or torch them on social media. When Volkswagen was playing up its commitment to building greener cars but got caught cheating on pollution emissions tests, its hypocrisy made the situation worse than the underlying crime. Sales tanked, and the company lost half its value. We can respect a company that walks the walk on the environment and can (perhaps grudgingly) accept a company that clearly doesn't give a damn. But the cognitive dissonance of saying one thing while doing another leads to catastrophic results.

Like Consumers, Brands Also Go on Journeys

It's worth repeating that brands can't simply *say* they're great anymore; they have to *be* great. That's been the guiding principle for what we do for our clients as an agency. The great irony is that we fell into the trap of image over execution because we didn't know how to execute properly. We were great in many ways when we rose to the top of the industry and won Agency of the Year, but we weren't great in every way. And that caused us to almost lose everything we had built. It wasn't an overt decision we made; it was a mistake born out of unpreparedness. We didn't have the processes, tools, and culture in place when we hit the vertical part of our exponential curve.

Just as customers go on journeys, so do brands. Exponential growth is incredibly hard, and only a small percentage of companies can obtain it. And only a small subset of those companies can maintain the momentum. After many years of the daily grinding that builds an army of evangelists, most don't realize that a different set of processes will be needed when exponential growth kicks in.

That's what happened with our agency. We delivered strong results for our clients, we built empowering content for the industry, and we had a small but mighty army of evangelists who loved our perspective on modern branding and advertising. Unfortunately we didn't have scalable processes that would ensure flawless execution when our growth started to explode. The lesson we learned is that brands must concurrently build out processes to manage exponential growth while building the empowering content and experiences that create it.

Purpose Drives All Decisions

Our agency's savior was supposed to be a gentleman we'll call Andrew. He's a former advertising executive with excellent connections to investors. The agencies that his new holding company were buying got nice paydays and access to new clients. He invited me up to his beautiful home outside of New York City, where I learned that some of what I had heard about him is true—that he's charming and intelligent. I had been warned about his downside, which is that he can't control his emotions and behavior, but I didn't experience it over lunch—that would come later.

As I drove home, I felt that even though there were warning signs, we were a good fit for each other. He could save us from the predicament that we were in, and our strong brand could help anchor his new holding company. The next part of the acquisition process was for me to meet with the investor who had flown in from China. Andrew had everything set up, and he just needed me to show some respect and charm. Check that box and the agency would be saved.

The meeting was set for 9 a.m. in New York City, about a two-and-a-half-hour drive from my weekend home in the Berkshires. I needed to leave at 6:30. To be safe, I left at 4:45. In pitch-black darkness, I was driving down the road when I heard the sickening flip, flip, flip of a busted tire as it banged against the wheel well of my station wagon.

Quickly, I ran the math and realized I should be okay. I pulled into the parking lot of a beautiful stone church that sits at a crossroads in the town. It was built in 1828, and the parking lot wasn't even paved. I pulled over, took out my phone to use as a flashlight, and found the jack. I was wearing my suit pants, which I didn't want to scuff up. So I pulled them off and neatly folded them and placed them on the seat of the car.

So there I am, a Jewish guy, naked except for his underwear at 4:30 in the morning, in the parking lot of a Presbyterian church, trying to do something I had not done in 20 years. As I cranked my jack, my hand repeatedly hit the ground. I was so filled with adrenaline that I didn't realize that every time I hit the mud, I was cutting my knuckles open.

I took out the lug wrench and put it on the nut. It wouldn't budge. Try as I might, I couldn't get the damn tire to come off. Adrenaline continued to flow. Profanities were echoing off the side of the stone church, but the lug nuts wouldn't loosen. I couldn't even tell if they were turning. I tried to mark them with a rock, but when that failed, I used the blood coming from my knuckles to create a vertical line so I could see if I was turning anything. Then I tried again and realized they weren't budging. I was just stripping the inside of the wrench.

I knew that if I didn't get this situation fixed quickly, traffic would build up and I would miss my meeting. I was out of cell range, so I couldn't make a call for help. Then I realized that I could probably make it to the train station. It was about 45 minutes away. That would bring me into Grand Central, and, chances are, I would be fine. I ran the math in my head. It was an easy model: I would cause about a thousand dollars in damage to the car in exchange for saving the agency. No-brainer. Let's roll.

I threw the jack and everything back in the car, pulled my pants back on, and headed to the nearest train station riding my rim. Sparks flew. The flapping got louder. I drove as steadily as I could as the car yawed sideways. After about 10 minutes, it became clear that the idea wouldn't work. The tire shredded so badly that it was getting stuck in the wheel well. There was no way I could drive on it for 35 minutes.

I pulled into a driveway so I wouldn't get hit by a truck on the narrow road. It was one of those rural parts of New York where there was only a driveway every few miles. It's hard to describe the dichotomy of the situation. On the one hand, I was on the verge of losing an agency that I had built up for 15 years with people that I truly loved. On the other, there was only one person on the planet I knew could save us. He was in New York City simply awaiting a handshake. I needed a miracle.

That miracle came in the form of the man who opened the door of the house whose driveway I just pulled into. He looked exactly like Robert Duvall. He had medium-length horseshoe hair circling his bald head and a giant cigar in his mouth, which he apparently enjoys at sunrise each day. He took one look at me and the car, and his eyes narrowed. "Can I help you?" he asked. And as it turns out, he may have been the only person who actually could. This character straight out of a Hollywood movie was a professional auto racing mechanic.

There was a racetrack nearby where rich guys drove vintage race cars on the weekends. His job was to keep those cars up and running. It turned out that I had pulled into the perfect driveway, at the perfect time, to meet the perfect guy to save me. The scene reminded me of Humphrey Bogart's iconic line from *Casablanca*, "Of all the gin joints, in all the towns, in all the world . . ." The mathematical chances of me pulling into this specific driveway were infinitesimally small. And yet, there I was.

Wordlessly, he turned his back to me, walked into a shed, and returned with a racing jack. I felt like an emasculated schmuck as he slid it under the car, but this was no time to listen to my ego. In three pumps, the rear wheel was off the ground. He grabbed my lug wrench, put it around the nut, and cranked it. I was actually relieved when it didn't work. At least it was the wrench that was the problem, not me. He looked up at me and said, "Well, these Swedish engineers must have their heads all the way up a cow's ass to design it this way." I felt slightly less emasculated.

He went back in his shed and emerged a few moments later with the same power tools you see pit crews use on TV. He removed the tire, put my spare on, released the car from the jack, and had the entire situation fixed in about two minutes. He never even removed the cigar from his mouth.

I was still going to be a bit late to the meeting, but I knew I could make them laugh with the incredible story of Robert Duvall and his cigar saving me in the middle of nowhere. The bloody knuckles were proof.

When I finally got to New York City, I looked the investor in the eye and gave him a great handshake. I smiled, laughed correctly, and told him the amazing story. The meeting went fine. At the conclusion, he said he liked me and that he wanted to complete the deal.

I drove back up to my house, where my wife was sitting on the front porch. I've been with her since college, and she's seen some weird behavior out of me before. I got out of the car, wearing my suit, which was still unwrinkled because the entire meeting had taken only an hour. "You're not going to believe this one," I told her as I pulled down my pants to reveal that I just came from a multimillion-dollar meeting with legs covered in mud and blood.

The deal didn't go through quickly. They never do. Meanwhile, we started making improvements to our agency. Jordan and I realized we needed help in operations and promoted a brilliant member of our team, Debbie Dumont, to managing director. With her help, we fixed our culture and strengthened our relationships with our clients. Soon, we were getting back to being a healthy agency with great people, great work, great clients, and great relationships.

At the same time, Andrew started to reveal his true self. He stressed out over the littlest things. He couldn't control his emotions. At one point, he called me while I was on vacation in Savannah, Georgia. I was getting ice cream with my kids. Generally speaking, I'm a workaholic and don't mind working excessive hours. But I also work my tail off when it comes to my family. They make a lot of sacrifices due to my workload, so ice cream on vacation is an untouchable time.

Still, the damn phone wouldn't stop buzzing. When I finally picked up, Andrew didn't have anything valuable to say. He was just stressing and talking in circles. I started to see what a nightmare it would be to work for him. I had a team that loved one another and clients who loved us. We were steadily working our way back to profitability and putting out great work. Most importantly, everyone was happy again. And I knew that Andrew was just the kind of guy who would screw that up.

At that point, I had a decision to make. There was a lot of money on the table, but I had spent my adulthood building up a company that I was enormously proud of. I worked with the best and brightest people I could find. Simply making money has never been my purpose. Building a great business and enjoying every single day at work is.

With the final negotiated contract in my hand, I walked away on signing day. It would have been the easy way out of a tough situation, but it was not what would make us happy.

Exponential Curves Require Preparation for Success

At Questus, we always knew that focus, purpose, culture, and team building were important. What we didn't realize was that exponential growth makes maintaining these core tenants much more challenging. As we reset our approach, we educated ourselves by reading books from some of the best and brightest. We read everything we could get our hands on and learned everything we could about operations, culture, and team building. But the best lesson didn't come from *Harvard Business Review*. It came from *Sports Illustrated*.

We read about a college coach named Joe Moglia. He had once been CEO of TD Ameritrade, which he helped grow exponentially from $24 billion in client assets to $280 billion, providing shareholders with a 500 percent return on investment. He did this after coaching high school and college football until he was 34, missing some prime years of business education.

At the peak of his career, he stepped down as CEO of TD Ameritrade to follow his life's passion again. After spending two years as an assistant for Nebraska, he took over as the head coach of Coastal Carolina University. Moglia quickly turned the team into the number one ranked team in the league. Not simply because of his football acumen, but because of the leadership skills he learned running TD Bank.

He leveraged data, operations, and empowerment. He looked at every facet of football competition and took a fresh approach, hammering it home with a quote that he painted on the wall: "The most dangerous phrase in the English language is, 'We've always done it this way.'"

His team rarely hit in practice, which cut down on injuries by 50 percent. Rather than have backups watch the first-team practice like virtually every other team did, he split the field to increase reps by 40 percent. He set aside extra time for special teams to create leverage, resulting in a 15-yard average differential in field position on kickoffs.

He also ensured that the team and staff were empowered for a balanced life, which is incredibly rare in NCAA football. Every week, he cut practice short by 30 minutes for a Life After Football session where the team discussed everything from racism and fatherhood to money management. Rather than instilling a workaholic culture for his staff, he insisted on maximizing efficiency throughout practice to ensure that the coaches got home to their families every evening. Empowerment permeated every aspect of the team's performance.

One anecdote stood out, in particular. It helped us realize exactly what was missing from our own playbook. Moglia built processes to manage every granular element of competition. Not just how practices are run, but for every situation in a game. For example, the coaches knew that when their placekicker missed a kick during the game, he was much more likely to miss again in the game. So they built a rule for game day that they would not have him kick again after a miss instead going for the first down. During a championship game, the kicker missed a field goal. But soon after, Moglia gave him another chance. He missed again, and the team lost.

What I found so enlightening was that Moglia wasn't tortured by the miss. He felt bad for the kid. What tortured him was that he had built a process that took emotions out of the 25-second time period to make a decision. He had every detail figured out in advance, but he didn't follow the plan.

The big lesson for us was to build processes to manage success. We weren't going to get by simply based on a vision and a team. We couldn't get by simply by having the right ideas and doing some great work. We needed to understand every aspect of success, and then document and manage those processes. Expertise is insufficient. Process creates scale. We needed to put everyone in position to do their best work, which is the definition of strong culture.

Exponential curves require processes and planning. When the growth curve is flat, decisions are relatively easy. Every day is fairly similar, but when the compound effect kicks in and the curve starts to rocket skyward, decisions are much bigger and more frequent. Navigating exponential growth successfully requires scalable processes. Moglia built his processes and found incredible success. When he failed to follow them, he lost a championship game. The same was true for my agency, and the same will be true for any brand not fully prepared for success.

After I turned down the buyout, we implemented scalable processes for recruiting the best talent in the industry and executing strategic assignments for some of the world's most influential brands. We launched Human Hug Project, for example, soon after the aborted buyout. Success bred more success, and each great project has enabled us to bring on even more talented people. Today, that's what we focus on first and foremost: hiring incredibly talented, kind, collaborative, passionate people who believe in our vision.

This has been the key to our growth and leads to the final lesson in this book, which is this: *Prepare for success.* Exponential curves are relatively flat and can lull a team to sleep before growth skyrockets vertically and forces dramatic change. Brands that are not prepared crash and burn.

Scalable Processes Facilitate Exponential Growth

In case you are not a sports fan, here's another example to help make this lesson tangible. Rodney Scott is a barbecue pitmaster whose career is a perfect example of how to handle an exponential curve. He grew up in South Carolina and went to work at his father's whole hog barbecue pit at 6 years old, with his first all-night smoke at 11 years old and a full-time job at 17.

Over decades, he learned how to create some of the world's best barbecue simply by feel. He didn't need to carefully measure out every recipe. He knew the proportions by eyeballing the spices in plastic containers. He didn't need to check the temperature of the fire; he knew it by simply hearing the pace of the rendered fat hitting the flames.

After three decades of painstaking work, including countless all-nighters and trees chopped down by hand, the culinary world took notice of Rodney. The *New York Times* wrote a glowing article about his family's restaurant. Soon after he won a prestigious award from the James Beard Foundation and was featured on Netflix and in the *Washington Post*. He partnered with an investor who turned his name into a brand and started growing exponentially with new restaurants throughout the Southeast. Each restaurant has lines out the door and an army of evangelists spreading the Rodney Scott brand name.

For Rodney, this growth required a fundamentally different approach to cooking. He couldn't get by on feel. He couldn't muscle through the day-to-day challenges. He needed processes to manage his exponential growth. So, he reverse-engineered everything he did. He figured out the exact measurements for his recipes, the exact temperatures for his fires, the exact timing for his cooks. He shifted from being a pitmaster to a coach and educator. He focused on finding the best talent available and then teaching the exact specifications for meeting his standards.

Just as Coach Moglia had processes for every practice scenario and game-day situation, Rodney Scott provides a great example of exactly how to handle exponential growth. When growth kicked in, Scott could have tried to keep doing more of the same. Or he could have leveraged processes from other restaurants only to see quality suffer. Instead, he worked painstakingly to document every granular element of success and ensure that his leaders could execute them properly. He didn't wait for exponential growth to kick in to develop these processes. When the curve kicked in, he had the processes in place. Growth without process is a toxic combination that Rodney avoided.

The lesson for brands is to build processes that manage every component of a business, right down to elements as small as grains of salt. At our agency, we built out processes for how we can attract the best talent in the industry and get them to collaborate effectively and efficiently. We built processes for how every one of our deliverables is created. We built a system for embracing transparency so every team member is aware of our successes and failures. We even built processes for how we would build out new processes as next-generation tools and technology emerge.

Like Rodney Scott and Joe Moglia, we didn't remove gut instincts. Rather, we built systems to document, share, and scale those instincts through institutional education. The same is true for all brands, regardless of industry or size. Process and training are what bring vision and ideas to life. No facet of competition is too small to document and optimize.

Empowerment Leads to Exponential Happiness

I'd like to inject a critical point that I've learned along my journey: Empowerment doesn't simply generate great business results. It also generates great personal results. Most of us got into marketing and advertising because we were looking for something more creative and more rewarding than we could find in other industries.

Study after study proves that happiness is primarily based on relationships. The stronger the relationships you have in life, the higher degree of happiness you generate. Money, fame, and power pale in comparison to the effect of healthy relationships. When you empower your customers, you build stronger relationships. When you empower a team, you build stronger relationships.

Today, I'm thankful for the moment when we lost our core focus on culture. It was brief, but the pain was incredibly instructive. It hurt not just me but also team members I love. It helped me fully understand the power of building relationships, not just between brands and customers but also within teams. I wasn't obtuse before our problems came. I always did my best to build a happy team, but that difficult experience helped me understand that attitude isn't nearly as important as execution.

When I figured out how, exactly, to empower my team, our business not only thrived, but I thrived as a human being. Empowerment leads to stronger relationships.

Stronger relationships lead to personal happiness. It's a simple but profound finding.

The Fourth Industrial Revolution Will Create Even More Exponential Change

Our human ancestors walked the earth for approximately 5 million years before finally using stone tools approximately 2.6 million years ago. Then, they spent over 2 million years foraging before finally starting to farm around 10,000 years ago. Only a small blip forward on a timeline and we created the first industrial revolution around 1760, during which agriculture was replaced by industry as the backbone of the economy. One quick century later, new sources of energy—electricity, gas, and oil—emerged to create the second industrial revolution. Almost exactly a century later, we saw the emergence of the third industrial revolution with electronics, telecommunications, and computers.

Now, we are entering into the fourth industrial revolution, fueled by automation, big data, and artificial intelligence. It is happening around us so quickly that we can feel it. A recent study by McKinsey found that in 1958, the average life span of companies in the S&P 500 was 61 years. Today, it is less than 18 years. McKinsey predicts that by 2027, 75 percent of the companies currently quoted on the S&P 500 will have disappeared.

Artificial intelligence has people like Bill Gates and Elon Musk losing sleep because it means computers are starting to have the power to emulate human thought and actually solve problems for themselves. Virtual and augmented reality as well as biotechnology are blurring the lines between human and computerized existence. Robotics may create changes as profound as the internet.

Each of these technologies will continue to change the relationship between brands and consumers. Brands will be even more transparent. Consumers will gain even more power and become even more demanding. The thirst for empowering content and experiences will grow, as will the disdain for interruptions and friction.

We have to accept that traditional techniques will become increasingly ineffective when the fourth industrial revolution kicks in. Instead of top-down patriarchal business models, we need nurturing, empowering ones. Instead of silos and rigidity, we need open-ended communication and collaboration. As brands, we need to give consumers tools to improve their lives. As employers, we need to put people in position to do their best work. And as everyday people, we need to seek out brands, jobs, and careers that not only serve us financially but also empower us to lead fulfilling lives. The rate of change is exponential, and so are the opportunities.

Three Exponential Takeaways

- Exponential curves are relatively flat and can lull a team to sleep before growth skyrockets vertically and forces dramatic change.

- After many years of grinding that builds an army of evangelists, most don't realize that a different set of processes will be needed when exponential growth kicks in.

- The rate of change is growing exponentially, and we are entering the fourth industrial revolution. Brands must prepare for even more rapid change.

And One Question to Ponder

If your brand doubled in size in the next year, would you have the processes and tools in place to maintain your culture and the quality of your products?

ACKNOWLEDGMENTS

It takes a village to write a book, and I would like to take this moment to thank some of the people involved.

- First and foremost, thank you to my family. I think the only thing more challenging than writing a book is living with someone who is writing a book. I love and appreciate you more than I can express in words.
- Thank you, every single member of the amazing Questus team, both past and present, as well as our incredible clients. You inspire me and humble me every single day. I am beyond fortunate to be surrounded by such kind, caring, and intelligent people on a daily basis.
- Thank you, Jordan Berg, for supporting me on yet another insane idea. I appreciate you and everything we have done together. What a ride it's been, partner.
- Thank you, Amy Li and Donya Dickerson at McGraw Hill, and my agent Jud Laghi, for seeing the vision

for the book and supporting me with strategic guidance throughout the entire development process. In particular, thank you, Amy, for the great advice that helped create a cohesive, actionable story.

- Thank you, Will Weisser and Joe Shepter, for helping write and edit the book. I marvel at how you turned my disparate thoughts into a cohesive narrative. I appreciate your expertise and the patience.

- Thank you, Nicole Scotten, for managing the book development process, helping me work through the toughest chapters, and leading all marketing initiatives. I could not have done this without you.

- Thank you, Jordan Berg, Jenny McLain, Justin Reynolds, Ted Herteg, Brady Brook, and Luke Kelly, for the cover design. I wish I had just one ounce of your talents.

- Thank you, Cristina Bermudez, for the research to ground my key points. Please remember that I was nice to you when you are running a Fortune 500 or the entire country.

- Thank you, Debbie Dumont, Emily Yates, Sherng-Lee Huang, and Frank Esposito, for reading early drafts and giving honest feedback about their shortcomings. This book would have been a hot mess without you.

- Thank you, Joe and Janet, for sharing your beautiful daughter with me. I couldn't write this book or do much of anything else without her.

- Thank you, Mom and Dad, for all of the business and advertising lessons we learned around the dinner table. And thank you for all of the trips to the bookstores in Vermont to teach me the power of a good book.

BIBLIOGRAPHY

Chapter 1: Introduction to the Advertising Revolution

- Graham Kendall, "Would Your Phone Be Powerful Enough to Get You to the Moon Like Apollo Did," *Business Standard*, October 2019, https://www.business-standard.com/article/technology/would-your-phone-be-powerful-enough-to-get-you-to-the-moon-like-apollo-did-119070200272_1.html.
- Nicole Roberts, "How Much Time Americans Spend in Front of Screens Will Terrify You," *Forbes*, July 16, 2021, https://www.forbes.com/sites/graisondangor/2021/07/16/pfizer-vaccine-has-goal-of-january-fda-approval/?sh=6fc7130b3049.
- Patricia Lauro, "The Media Business: Advertising; Whassup? America's Asking," *New York Times*, February 16, 2021, https://www.nytimes.com/2001/02/16/business/the-media-business-advertising-whassup-america-s-asking.html.
- Agnieska Guttman, "Advertising Spending in North America from 2000 to 2022," Statista, June 2, 2021, https://www.statista.com/statistics/429036/advertising-expenditure-in-north-america/.
- Katie Jones, "How Total Spend by U.S. Advertisers Has Changed, Over 20 Years," *Visual Capitalist*, October 16, 2020, https://www.visualcapitalist.com/us-advertisers-spend-20-years/.
- Tony Schwartz, "Companies That Practice 'Conscious Capitalism,' Perform 10x Better" *Harvard Business Review*, April 2013, https://hbr.org/2013/04/companies-that-practice-conscious-capitalism-perform.
- Will Kenton, "Conscious Capitalism," April 21, 2018, Investopedia, https://www.investopedia.com/terms/c/conscious-capitalism.asp.
- Jeff Kauflin, "Feel Good, Get Rich with New Goldman Sachs Paul Tudor Jones ETF," June 2018, *Forbes*, https://www.forbes.com/sites/jeffkauflin/2018/06/13/feel-good-get-rich-with-new-goldman-sachs-paul-tudor-jones-etf/?sh=78af716d6a5c.

- Matthew Heimer, "Why a Data Revolution Is Giving Socially Responsible Investors an Edge," September 2019, *Fortune*, https://fortune.com/2019/09/25/esg-investing-stocks-data-revolution/.
- David B. Wolfe, Jagdish Sheth, and Rajendra Sisodia, *Firms of Endearment: How World-Class Companies Profit from Passion and Purpose* (Pearson, 2014).
- Global Justice Now, "69 of the Richest 100 Entities on the Planet Are Corporations, Not Governments, Figures Show," Global Justice Now, October 17, 2018, https://www.globaljustice.org.uk/news/69-richest-100-entities-planet-are-corporations-not-governments-figures-show/.
- Global Justice Now, "10 Biggest Corporations Make More Money Than Most Countries in the World Combined," *Global Justice Now*, September 12, 2016, https://www.globaljustice.org.uk/news/10-biggest-corporations-make-more-money-most-countries-world-combined/.
- Evan Bakker, "Shopping Cart Abandonment: Merchants Now Leave $4.6 Trillion on the Table, and Mobile Is Making the Problem Worse," *Business Insider*, November 15, 2016, https://www.businessinsider.com/shopping-cart-abandonment-merchants-now-leave-46-trillion-on-the-table-and-mobile-is-making-the-problem-worse-2016-11.
- Louise Story, "Anywhere the Eye Can See, It's Likely to See an Ad," *New York Times*, January 15, 2007, https://www.nytimes.com/2007/01/15/business/media/15everywhere.html.
- Amelia Lucas, "Here Are the Biggest Super Bowl Advertisers of the Last 11 Years," CNBC, February 6, 2021, https://www.cnbc.com/2021/02/06/here-are-the-biggest-super-bowl-advertisers-of-the-last-11-years.html.
- Jan Conway, "Global Market Share of the Leading Beer Companies in 2019, Based on Volume Sales," Statista, October 12, 2020, https://www.statista.com/statistics/257677/global-market-share-of-the-leading-beer-companies-based-on-sales/.
- Autotrader, "2020 Cox Automotive Car Buyer Journey," Autotrader, 2020, https://b2b.autotrader.com/app/uploads/2020-Car-Buyer-Journey-Study.pdf.
- Wayne Elsey, "Why Your Company Should Be More Socially Responsible," *Forbes*, May 30, 2018, https://www.forbes.com/sites/forbesbusinessdevelopmentcouncil/2018/05/30/why-your-company-should-be-more-socially-responsible/?sh=30217f2b2c32.

- Business.com editorial staff, "Can You Make a Profit and Be Socially Responsible?" Business.com, April 8, 2020, https://www.business.com/articles/can-you-make-a-profit-and-be-socially-responsible/.
- Robert G. Eccles, "The Impact of Corporate Sustainability on Organizational Processes and Performance," Informs, November 6, 2014, https://pubsonline.informs.org/doi/abs/10.1287/mnsc.2014.1984.
- Beiting Cheng, Ioannis Ioannou, and George Serafeim, "Corporate Social Responsibility and Access to Finance," April 5, 2013, https://onlinelibrary.wiley.com/doi/abs/10.1002/smj.2131.
- Maureen Kline, "How Corporate Responsibility Can Deliver ROI," Inc., July 9, 2015, https://www.inc.com/maureen-kline/how-corporate-responsibility-can-deliver-roi.html.
- Accenture, "The Bottom Line on Business Trust," Accenture, 2018, https://www.accenture.com/_acnmedia/Thought-Leadership-Assets/PDF/Accenture-Competitive-Agility-Index.pdf.
- Andrew Zimmerman Jones, "Understanding Momentum in Physics," ThoughtCo., November 24, 2019, https://www.thoughtco.com/what-is-momentum-2698743.
- Wikipedia, "Exponential Growth," Wikipedia, https://en.wikipedia.org/wiki/Exponential_growth.
- Selena Maranjian, "Compound Interest and Compounding Growth: A Comprehensive Guide," The Motley Fool, May 24, 2019, https://www.fool.com/retirement/2018/07/10/compound-interest-and-compounding-growth-a-compreh.aspx.
- Mckenna Moore, "Stakeholder Capitalism: Is It Working, or Is It All Talk?" *Fortune*, November 3, 2020, https://fortune.com/2020/11/03/stakeholder-capitalism-lucian-bebchuk-rebecca-henderson-business-roundtable/.
- Tony Schwartz, "Companies That Practice 'Conscious Capitalism' Perform 10x Better," *Harvard Business Review*, April 4, 2013, https://hbr.org/2013/04/companies-that-practice-conscious-capitalism-perform.
- Rajendra Sisodia, "Doing Business in the Age of Conscious Capitalism," ResearchGate, June 2009, https://www.researchgate.net/publication/235252046_Doing_business_in_the_age_of_conscious_capitalism.
- Fortune Staff, "Big Companies Join Vatican-Affiliated Council Pledging Inclusive Capitalism," *Fortune*, December 7, 2020, https://fortune.com/2020/12/08/council-for-inclusive-capitalism-with-the-vatican/.

- Catherine Yoshimoto and Ed Frauenheim, "The Best Companies to Work for Are Beating the Market," *Fortune*, February 27, 2018, https://fortune.com/2018/02/27/the-best-companies-to-work-for-are -beating-the-market/.
- Mike Snider, "Budweiser Falls from Top Three U.S. Beer Favorites," *USA Today*, January 24, 2018, https://www.usatoday.com /story/money/food/2018/01/23/budweiser-falls-top-three-u-s-beer -favorites/1057374001/.
- Ioannis Ioannou, "Why It Pays to Be Socially Responsible in Business," London Business School, July 4, 2018, https://www.london .edu/think/why-it-pays-to-be-socially-responsible-in-business.

Chapter 2: Modern Advertising Is a Value Exchange

- Jack Neff, "Study: 80% of Super Bowl Ads Don't Help Sales," January 6, 2014, *Ad Age*, https://adage.com/article/special-report-super-bowl /study-80-super-bowl-ads-sales/290907.
- Avery Yang, "How Much Does a Super Bowl Commercial Cost," *Sports Illustrated*, February 2, 2020, https://www.si.com/nfl/2020 /02/02/how-much-does-super-bowl-commercial-cost-history-2020.
- Guttman, "Advertising Market Worldwide—Statistics & Facts," Statista, January 15, 2021, https://www.statista.com/topics/990 /global-advertising-market/.
- "Consumer Trust in Online, Social and Mobile Advertising Grows," Nielsen, April 11, 2012, https://www.nielsen.com/us/en /insights/article/2012/consumer-trust-in-online-social-and-mobile -advertising-grows/.
- Akville Defazio, "How Much Do Instagram Ads Cost in 2021? (+ How to Make the Most of Your Budget)," Wordstream, July 12, 2021, https://www.wordstream.com/blog/ws/2021/02/08/instagram-ads -cost.
- "How Much Does Facebook Advertising Cost in 2021," Webfx, January 2021, https://www.webfx.com/social-media/how-much-does -facebook-advertising-cost.html.
- "How Much Money Does It Cost to Advertise on Twitter," Webfx, https://www.webfx.com/social-media/how-much-does-it-cost-to -advertise-on-twitter.html.

- "Online Media Kit," *New York Times*, https://archive.nytimes.com /www.nytimes.com/partners/microsites/oct/nytodaymediakit/rates .html.
- Tim Fitzpatrick, "How Much Does It Cost to Advertise on Twitter," Rialto Marketing, August 3, 2020, https://www.rialtomarketing.com /how-much-does-cost-advertise-twitter/.
- Kristina Monllos, "What a $5.6m Super Bowl Buy Can Purchase in Digital Media in 2020," Digiday, January 30, 2020, https://digiday .com/marketing/5-6m-super-bowl-buy-can-purchase-digital -media-2020/
- Soma Biswas and Suzanne Kapner, "J.Crew Tumbles into Bankruptcy in the Wake of Coronavirus," *Wall Street Journal*, May 4, 2020, https://www.wsj.com/articles/j-crew-files-for-bankruptcy-protection -reaches-debt-swap-deal-11588583196.
- Jennifer Spencer, "How to Use 'the Law of Reciprocity' to Build Better Business Relationships," *Entrepreneur*, March 21, 2019, https://www .entrepreneur.com/article/330557.
- Michael Glover, "Word of Mouth Marketing in 2021: How to Create a Strategy for Social Media Buzz & Skyrocket Referral Sales," BigCommerce, https://www.bigcommerce.com/blog/word-of-mouth -marketing/#word-of-mouth-marketing-statistics.
- Dominic-Madori Davis, "Gen Zers Have a Spending Power of Over $140 Billion, and It's Driving the Frenzy of Retailers and Brands Trying to Win Their Dollars," *Business Insider*, January 28, 2020, https://www.businessinsider.com/retail-courts-gen-z-spending -power-over-140-billion-2020-1.
- Ruth N. Bolton, "Marketing Renaissance: Opportunities and Imperatives for Improving Marketing Thought, Practice, and Infrastructure," *Sage Journals*, October 1, 2005, https://journals .sagepub.com/doi/10.1509/jmkg.2005.69.4.1.
- Lucian Bebchuk and Roberto Tallarita, "The Illusory Promise of Stakeholder Governance," Harvard Law School Forum on Corporate Governance, September 2, 2021, https://corpgov.law.harvard.edu /2020/03/02/the-illusory-promise-of-stakeholder-governance/.
- Guy Brusselmans, John Blasberg, and James Root, "The Biggest Contributor to Brand Growth," Bain & Company, March 19, 2014, https://www.bain.com/insights/the-biggest-contributor-to-brand -growth/.

Chapter 3: This Is Your Brain on Advertising

- Paul J. Zak, *Trust Factor: The Science Behind Creating High-Performance Companies* (AMACOM Books, 2017).
- Walter Isaacson, *Steve Jobs* (Simon & Schuster, 2011).
- David B. Wolfe, Jagdish Sheth, and Rajendra Sisodia, *Firms of Endearment: How World-Class Companies Profit from Passion and Purpose* (Pearson, 2014).
- John Medina, *Brain Rules* (Pear Press, 2008).
- Christopher Chabris and Daniel Simons, *The Invisible Gorilla* (MJF Books, 2010).
- Paul J. Zak, *The Moral Molecule: How Trust Works* (Plume, 2013).
- TED, "Paul Zak: Trust, Morality—and Oxytocin," YouTube, November 1, 2011, https://www.youtube.com/watch?v=rFAdlU2ETjU &t=242s.
- Roger Dooley, *FRICTION—the Untapped Force That Can Be Your Most Powerful Advantage* (McGraw-Hill Education, 2019).
- Future of Storytelling, "Future of StoryTelling: Paul Zak," YouTube, February 19, 2013, https://www.youtube.com/watch?v=DHeqQAKHh3M.
- J. B. Maverick, "If You Purchased $100 of Apple in 2002," Investopedia, April 14, 2019, https://www.investopedia.com/articles/markets/021316/if-you-had-purchased-100-apple-2002-aapl.asp.
- Dr. Saul McLeod, "Theories of Selective Attention," SimplyPsychology, 2018, https://www.simplypsychology.org/attention-models.html.
- Jon Hamilton, "Why Brain Scientists Are Still Obsessed with the Curious Case of Phineas Gage," NPR, May 21, 2017, https://www.npr.org/sections/health-shots/2017/05/21/528966102/why-brain-scientists-are-still-obsessed-with-the-curious-case-of-phineas-gage.
- Paul Zak, "Why Inspiring Stories Make Us React: The Neuroscience of Narrative," *Cerebrum* (2015): https://www.ncbi.nlm.nih.gov/pmc/articles/PMC4445577/.
- Daniel Tranel, "Prefrontal Cortex Damage Abolishes Brand-Cued Changes in Cola Preference," *Social Cognitive and Affective Neuroscience*, March 3, 2008, https://www.ncbi.nlm.nih.gov/pmc/articles/PMC2288573/.
- Will Wei, "We Re-created the Pepsi Challenge to See What People Really Like," *Business Insider*, May 3, 2013, https://www.businessinsider.com/pepsi-challenge-business-insider-2013-5.

- "The Pepsi Challenge: How Neuroscience Discovered the Hidden Truth," NeuroSenum, March 13, 2018, https://medium.com/@neurosensum/the-pepsi-challenge-how-neuroscience-discovered-the-hidden-truth-e5da7997f046.
- Mind Matters, "Working Memory: They Found Your Brain's Spam Filter," *Scientific American*, January 28, 2008, https://blogs.scientificamerican.com/news-blog/working-memory-they-found-your-brai/.
- Jordana Cepelewicz, "What a New Theory of Attention Says About Consciousness," *Atlantic*, September 29, 2019, https://www.theatlantic.com/science/archive/2019/09/how-brain-helps-you-pay-attention/598846/.
- Cepelewicz, Jordana, "To Pay Attention, the Brain Uses Filters, Not a Spotlight," *Quanta Magazine*, September 2019, https://www.quantamagazine.org/to-pay-attention-the-brain-uses-filters-not-a-spotlight-20190924/.
- Mind Matters "Working Memory: They Found Your Brain's Spam Filter" January 2008, https://blogs.scientificamerican.com/news-blog/working-memory-they-found-your-brai/.
- Jaime Netzer, "The Top Millennial Buying Habits and Insights for 2021," Khoros, July 01, 2020, https://khoros.com/blog/millennial-buying-habits.
- Dominic Davis, "Gen Zers Have a Spending Power of Over $140 Billion, and It's Driving the Frenzy of Retailers and Brands Trying to Win Their Dollars," *Business Insider*, January 28, 2020, https://www.businessinsider.com/retail-courts-gen-z-spending-power-over-140-billion-2020-1.
- Emmie Martin, "If You Invested $1,000 in Apple at Its IPO, Here's How Much Money You'd Have Now," CNBC, November 1, 2018, https://www.cnbc.com/2018/11/01/how-much-a-1000-dollar-investment-in-apple-at-its-ipo-would-be-worth-now.html.
- "Apple Market Cap," Ycharts, https://ycharts.com/companies/AAPL/market_cap.
- Amy Lamare, "How Warby Parker Disrupted the Eyewear Industry," Business of Business, October 6, 2020, https://www.businessofbusiness.com/articles/history-of-warby-parker-jobs-data/.
- Mark Honigsbaum, "Oxytocin: Could the 'Trust Hormone' Rebound Our Troubled World?" *Guardian*, August 2011, https://www.theguardian.com/science/2011/aug/21/oxytocin-zak-neuroscience-trust-hormone.

- Carl Zimmer, "100 Trillion Connections: New Efforts Probe and Map the Brain's Detailed Architecture," *Scientific American*, January 2011, https://www.scientificamerican.com/article/100-trillion-connections/.
- Daniel J. Levitin, "Why It's So Hard to Pay Attention, Explained by Science," Fast Company, September 23, 2015, https://www.fastcompany.com/3051417/why-its-so-hard-to-pay-attention-explained-by-science.
- David B. T. McMahon and Carl R. Olson, "Repetition Suppression in Monkey Inferotemporal Cortex: Relation to Behavioral Priming," *Journal of Neurophysiology*, May 1, 2007, https://journals.physiology.org/doi/full/10.1152/jn.01042.2006.
- A. K. Pradeep, *The Buying Brain: Secrets for Selling to the Subconscious Mind* (New Jersey: Wiley, 2010).
- Rebecca Ramirez, "Understanding Unconscious Bias," NPR, July 15, 2020, https://www.npr.org/2020/07/14/891140598/understanding-unconscious-bias.
- Jordan Gaines Lewis, "This Is How the Brain Filters out Unimportant Details," *Psychology Today*, February 11, 2015, https://www.psychologytoday.com/us/blog/brain-babble/201502/is-how-the-brain-filters-out-unimportant-details.
- Jordana Cepelewicz, "To Pay Attention, the Brain Uses Filters, Not a Spotlight," *Quanta Magazine*, September 24, 2019, https://www.quantamagazine.org/to-pay-attention-the-brain-uses-filters-not-a-spotlight-20190924/.
- Dothetest, "Test Your Awareness: Do the Test," YouTube, https://www.youtube.com/watch?v=Ahg6qcgoay4.
- Dothetest, "Test Your Awareness: Whodunnit?" YouTube, https://www.youtube.com/watch?v=ubNF9QNEQLA.
- Meg Selig, "The Amazing Power of 'Small Wins,'" *Psychology Today*, July 18, 2012, https://www.psychologytoday.com/us/blog/changepower/201207/the-amazing-power-small-wins.
- Kevin McSpadden, "You Now Have a Shorter Attention Span Than a Goldfish," *Time*, May 14, 2015, https://time.com/3858309/attention-spans-goldfish/.
- Faris Yakob, "The Goldfish Myth," WARC, August 31, 2018, https://www.warc.com/newsandopinion/opinion/the-goldfish-myth/2806.
- Warby Parker, "Impact Parker 2019," Warby Parker, https://www.warbyparker.com/assets/img/impact-report/Impact-Report-2019.pdf.

- Megan Kauffma, "Neil Blumenthal Shares the Warby Parker Story," *Wharton Magazine*, May 10, 2013, https://magazine.wharton.upenn.edu/digital/neil-blumenthal-shares-the-warby-parker-story/.
- Jason Del Rey, "An Unlikely Startup Enters the Point-of-Sale Business: Warby Parker," All Things D, June 24, 2013, https://allthingsd.com/20130624/an-unlikely-startup-enters-the-point-of-sale-business-warby-parker/.
- Heather Haddon and Preetika Rana, "Those Cosmic Wings You Had Delivered? They're Really from Applebee's," *Wall Street Journal*, March 28, 2021, https://www.wsj.com/articles/those-cosmic-wings-you-had-delivered-theyre-really-from-applebees-11616940000.
- Paul J. Zak, "The Neurobiology of Trust," *Scientific American*, https://www.scientificamerican.com/article/the-neurobiology-of-trust/.

Chapter 4: Your Brand Is Your Most Important Asset

- Scott Harrison, *Thirst* (Crown Publishing Group, 2020).
- LeWeb, "Scott Harrison, Founder & CEO, Charity: Water Shares His Story at LeWeb Paris 2012," YouTube, December 4, 2012, https://www.youtube.com/watch?v=XLdDMDkwK1s.
- NYU Entrepreneurial Institute, "Check out Scott Harrison's Keynote Speech at the NYU Entrepreneurs Festival," YouTube, June 29, 2017, https://www.youtube.com/watch?v=5XFlEm0YoHo.
- Walter Isaacson, *Steve Jobs* (Simon & Schuster, 2011), https://www.charitywater.org/.
- CreativeMornings HQ, "Scott Harrison: The Story of Charity : Water," YouTube, April 15, 2019, https://www.youtube.com/watch?v=z5a8KtUE1S4.
- North Point Community Church, "The Charity Water Story | SCOTT HARRISON," YouTube, July 26, 2017, https://www.youtube.com/watch?v=w8QdFdtsmbs.
- Louise Story, "Anywhere the Eye Can See, It's Likely to See an Ad," *New York Times*, January 15, 2007, https://www.nytimes.com/2007/01/15/business/media/15everywhere.html.
- Wikipedia, "Paul Rand," Wikipedia.org, https://en.wikipedia.org/wiki/Paul_Rand.
- Envato, "Paul Rand and the Stories Behind the World's Most Famous Logos," Envato, March 13, 2018, https://envato.com/blog/paul-rand-designing-famous-logos/.

- "Discover Kantar Brandz," Kantar, https://www.kantar.com/campaigns/brandz/global.
- Statista Research Department, "Coca-Cola's Brand Value from 2006 to 2021," Statista, 2021, https://www.statista.com/statistics/326065/coca-cola-brand-value/.
- Marty Swant, "The World's Most Valuable Brands," *Forbes*, https://www.forbes.com/the-worlds-most-valuable-brands/#103cb1ca119c.
- Statista Research Department, "Most Valuable Brands Worldwide in 2021," Statista, January 29, 2021, https://www.statista.com/statistics/264875/brand-value-of-the-25-most-valuable-brands/.
- Jon Simpson, "Finding Brand Success in the Digital World," *Forbes*, July 6, 2021, https://www.forbes.com/sites/officedepotofficemax/2021/07/06/her-bookstore-survived-the-pandemic-by-closing-its-doors--building-new-skills/?sh=61d4b6c07773.
- David Disalvo, "Your Brain Sees Even When You Don't," *Forbes*, June, 2013, https://www.forbes.com/sites/daviddisalvo/2013/06/22/your-brain-sees-even-when-you-dont/?sh=6588224e116a.
- Ted Kitterman, "Report: 83% of Millennials Want Brands to Align with Them on Values," *PR Daily*, December 28, 2020, https://www.prdaily.com/report-83-of-millennials-want-brands-to-align-with-them-on-values/.
- Gale Siegel, "Realize the Power of Simplicity," Siegel + Gale, January, 2017, https://www.siegelgale.com/realize-the-power-of-simplicity/.
- Nat Ives, "Average Tenure of CMOs Falls Again," *Wall Street Journal*, May, 2020, https://www.wsj.com/articles/average-tenure-of-cmos-falls-again-11590573600.
- Derrick Daye, "Great Moments in Branding: Neil McElroy Memo," Branding Strategy Insider, June 12, 2009, https://www.brandingstrategyinsider.com/great-moments-in-branding-neil-mcelroy-memo/#.YRbWuRNKg6E.
- Businesswire, "P&G Announces Fourth Quarter and Fiscal Year 2020 Results," Businesswire, July 30, 2020, https://www.businesswire.com/news/home/20200730005458/en/PG-Announces-Fourth-Quarter-and-Fiscal-Year-2020-Results.
- Andy Brownfield, "A Look at Procter & Gamble's Billion-Dollar Brands, Including Some Made in Triad," *Business Journals*, October 17, 2020, https://www.bizjournals.com/triad/news/2020/10/17/these-are-p-gs-billion-dollar-brands.html.
- Forbes, "World's Most Valuable Brands 2020," *Forbes*, July 27, 2020, https://www.forbes.com/companies/pepsi/?sh=4f05d1eabc31.

- Marty Swant, "The World's Most Valuable Brands," *Forbes*, https://www.forbes.com/the-worlds-most-valuable-brands/#e0758cd119c0.
- Aaron O'Neill, "Russia: Gross Domestic Product (GDP) in Current Prices from 1996 to 2026," Statista, May 19, 2021, https://www.statista.com/statistics/263772/gross-domestic-product-gdp-in-russia/.
- Colin Mayer, *Prosperity: Better Business Makes the Greater Good* (Oxford: Oxford University Press, 2018).
- Ocean Tomo, "Intangible Asset Market Value Study," Ocean Tomo, https://www.oceantomo.com/intangible-asset-market-value-study/.
- Soo Youn, "Nike Sales Booming After Colin Kaepernick Ad, Invalidating Critics," ABC News, December 21, 2018, https://abcnews.go.com/Business/nike-sales-booming-kaepernick-ad-invalidating-critics/story?id=59957137.
- Gina Martinez, "Despite Outrage, Nike Sales Increased 31% After Kaepernick Ad," *Time*, September 10, 2018, https://time.com/5390884/nike-sales-go-up-kaepernick-ad/.
- Timothy Bella, "'Just Do It': The Surprising and Morbid Origin Story of Nike's Slogan," *Washington Post*, September 4, 2018, https://www.washingtonpost.com/news/morning-mix/wp/2018/09/04/from-lets-do-it-to-just-do-it-how-nike-adapted-gary-gilmores-last-words-before-execution/.
- Branding Strategy Insider, https://www.brandingstrategyinsider.com/origins-of-brand-management/.
- Kate Taylor, "A Handful of Companies Control Almost Everything We Buy—and Beer Is the Latest Victim," Business Insider, August 24, 2017, https://www.businessinsider.com/companies-control-everything-we-buy-2017-8.
- Katie Jones, "Ranked: The Most Valuable Brands in the World," Visual Capitalist, January 30, 2020, https://www.visualcapitalist.com/ranked-the-most-valuable-brands-in-the-world/.
- Accenture, "The Bottom Line of Business Trust," Accenture, https://www.accenture.com/_acnmedia/Thought-Leadership-Assets/PDF/Accenture-Competitive-Agility-Index.pdf.
- Nora Xu and Kelli Kemery, "Maximizing Purchase Consideration Through the Trust Curve," Microsoft Advertising Blog, May 20, 2020, https://about.ads.microsoft.com/en-us/blog/post/may-2020/maximizing-purchase-consideration-through-the-trust-curve.

Chapter 5: Leveraging the Consumer Journey

- PBS News, "The Human Hug Project," August 2016, https://www.pbs
.org/video/wgvu-newsmakers-human-hug-project-1621/\.
- Barbara Peterson, "Consumers Visit 38 Sites Before Booking,
Expedia Says," Travel Market Report, December 2, 2015, https://
www.travelmarketreport.com/articles/Consumers-Visit-38-Sites
-Before-Booking-Expedia-Says.
- Masterclass Staff, "Writing 101: What Is the Hero's Journey? 2
Hero's Journey Examples in Film," Masterclass, November 8, 2020,
https://www.masterclass.com/articles/writing-101-what-is-the-heros
-journey.
- Dan Bronzite, "The Hero's Journey—Mythic Structure of Joseph
Campbell's Monomyth," Movie Outline, http://www.movieoutline
.com/articles/the-hero-journey-mythic-structure-of-joseph
-campbell-monomyth.html.
- Veteran Affairs, "Veteran Suicide Data and Reporting," Mental
Health, https://www.mentalhealth.va.gov/suicide_prevention/data
.asp.
- Nikki Wentling, "VA Reveals Its Veteran Suicide Statistic Included
Active-Duty Troops," Stripes, June 21, 2018, https://www.stripes.com
/theaters/us/va-reveals-its-veteran-suicide-statistic-included-active
-duty-troops-1.533992.
- Questus, "Can a Hug Save a Life?" https://www.questus.com/super8.
- Jay Price, "The Number 22: Is There a 'False Narrative' for Vet Suicide?"
NPR, October 1, 2015, https://www.npr.org/2015/10/01/444999996
/the-number-22-is-there-a-false-narrative-for-vet-suicide.
- Jeremy Ramirez, "A Review of Art Therapy Among Military Service
Members and Veterans with Post-Traumatic Stress Disorder,"
JMVH, https://jmvh.org/article/a-review-of-art-therapy-among
-military-service-members-and-veterans-with-post-traumatic-stress
-disorder/.
- Autotrader, "2020 CoxOX AUTOMOTIVE CAR BUYER JOURNEY,"
Autotrader, 2020, https://b2b.autotrader.com/app/uploads/2020-Car
-Buyer-Journey-Study.pdf.

Chapter 6: The Why and How of Culture

- Geoff Smart, *Who* (Ballantine Books, 2008).
- Daniel Coyle, *The Culture Code: The Secrets of Highly Successful
Groups* (Bantam, 2018).

- Runner's World, "This Is Why Kipchoge Smiles When He Runs (and Why You Should Be Doing It Too)," *Runner's World*, February 11, 2018, https://www.runnersworld.com/uk/training/motivation/a776539/how-smiling-improves-your-running/.
- Walter Isaacson and Steve Jobs (Simon & Schuster, 2011).
- Lisa Rowen, "Whatever Happened to American Apparel?" Glossy, January 2021, https://www.glossy.co/fashion/what-ever-happened-to-american-apparel/.
- Kurt Eichenwald, "Microsoft's Lost Decade'," *Vanity Fair*, August, 2012, https://archive.vanityfair.com/article/2012/8/microsofts-lost-decade.
- Alex Edmans, *Grow the Pie*, Cambridge University Press, Kindle edition.
- Marcel Schwantes, "Research: Why 70 Percent of Employees Aren't Working to Their Full Potential Comes Down to 1 Simple Reason" Inc., November 2017, https://www.inc.com/marcel-schwantes/research-why-70-percent-of-employees-arent-working-to-their-full-potential-comes-down-to-1-simple-reason.html.
- Kim Cameron, "Proof That Positive Work Cultures Are More Productive," HBR, December 1, 2015, https://hbr.org/2015/12/proof-that-positive-work-cultures-are-more-productive.
- Catherine Yoshimoto, "The Best Companies to Work for Are Beating the Market," *Fortune*, February 27, 2018, https://fortune.com/2018/02/27/the-best-companies-to-work-for-are-beating-the-market/.
- Sandra Burmeister, "How Employee Engagement Drives Customer Satisfaction," N2 Growth, https://www.n2growth.com/how-employee-engagement-drives-customer-satisfaction/.
- Donald Sull, "Measuring Cultures in Leading Communities," *Sloan Review*, June 24, 2019, https://sloanreview.mit.edu/projects/measuring-culture-in-leading-companies/.
- Daniel Ku, "26 Employee Engagement Statistics Every Manager Needs to Know," Post Beyond, July 7, 2020, https://www.postbeyond.com/blog/26-employee-engagement-stats/.
- "Does Corporate Culture Drive Financial Performance?" *Forbes*, February 10, 2011, https://www.forbes.com/sites/johnkotter/2011/02/10/does-corporate-culture-drive-financial-performance/?sh=29b7c81a7e9e.
- Heidi Kurter, "4 Strategies to Repair a Toxic Culture from the Top Down," *Forbes*, https://www.forbes.com/sites/heidilynnekurter/2019/12/23/4-strategies-to-repair-a-toxic-culture-from-the-top-down/?sh=794aa48e40e0.

- Isis Briones, "How Fender Helped Over 1 Million People Through Music During the Pandemic," *Forbes*, April 30, 2020, https://www .forbes.com/sites/isisbriones/2020/04/30/fender-play-app-one -million-giveaway/?sh=6379e61f2041.
- Leslie A. Perlow, "Stop the Meeting Madness," *Harvard Business Review*, August 2017, https://hbr.org/2017/07/stop-the-meeting -madness.
- Inc., "Brands and Brand Names," Inc., August 2021, https://www.inc .com/encyclopedia/brands-and-brand-names.html.
- Russell Hotten, "Volkswagen: The Scandal Explained," BBC, December 10, 2015, https://www.bbc.com/news/business-34324772.
- Sloan Review, "The Big 9 Cultural Values," *Sloan Review*, https:// sloanreview.mit.edu/culture500.
- John R. Graham, Campbell R. Harvey, Jillian Popadak, and Shivaram Rajgopal, "Corporate Culture: Evidence from the Field," National Bureau of Economic Research, March 2017, https://www.nber.org /papers/w23255.
- Kaplan, "The Impact of Organizational Culture on Business Success," Kaplan, https://www.kaplansolutions.com/article/the-impact-of -organizational-culture-on-business-success.
- John Noble Wilford, "When Humans Became Human," *New York Times*, February 26, 2002, https://www.nytimes.com/2002/02/26 /science/when-humans-became-human.html?.?mc=aud_dev&ad -keywords=auddevgate&gclid=Cj0KCQjw7MGJBhD-ARIsAMZ0e evoBjRm7Ct4qdhPpxljScyyDSIce9drALljLlhUiS4S2FGokIDjuqQa AtQxEALw_wcB&gclsrc=aw.ds.

Chapter 7: Selling the Big Idea

- John Medina, *Brain Rules* (Pear Press, 2008).
- Oren Klaff, *Pitch Anything: An Innovative Method for Presenting, Persuading, and Winning the Deal* (McGraw Hill, 2011).
- Daniel H. Pink, *To Sell Is Human: The Surprising Truth About Moving Others* (New York: Riverhead Books, 2013).
- Masterclass, "Daniel Pink Teaches Sales and Persuasion," Masterclass, https://www.masterclass.com/classes/daniel-pink-teaches-sales-and -persuasion.
- Future of Storytelling, "Future of StoryTelling: Paul Zak," YouTube, February 19, 2013, https://www.youtube.com/watch?v= DHeqQAKHh3M.

- Sheila Mclear, "This Exact Percentage of People Regularly Bring Their Phones into the Bathroom," The Ladders, November, 2019, https://www.theladders.com/career-advice/this-exact-percentage-of-people -regularly-bring-their-phones-into-the-bathroom.
- Amy Watson, "Media Use—Statistics & Facts," Statista, March 23, 2020, "https://www.statista.com/topics/1536/media-use/.
- Chloe Tejada, "Why Your Phone Shouldn't Be a Part of Your Morning Routine," *Huffington Post*, December 12, 2019, https://www.huffingtonpost.ca/entry/dont-check-phone-in-morning_ca _5df24c1ae4b01e0f295b6d0a.
- N. Mendoza, "66% of Americans Admit to Sleeping with Their Phone at Night," Tech Republic, February 20, 2020, https://www.techrepublic.com/article/66-of-americans-admit-to-sleeping-with -their-phone-at-night/.
- Henry Blodget, "90% of 18–29 Year-Olds Sleep with Their Smartphones" *Business Insider*, November 21, 2012, https://www.businessinsider.com/90-of-18-29-year-olds-sleep-with-their -smartphones-2012-11.
- Rochi Zalani, "Screen Time Statistics 2021: Your Smartphone Is Hurting You," Elite Content Marketer, June 2, 2021, https://elitecontentmarketer.com/screen-time-statistics/.
- "Study Reveals Brain's Finely Tuned System of Energy Supply," URMC, August 2016, https://www.urmc.rochester.edu/news/story /study-reveals-brains-finely-tuned-system-of-energy-supply.
- Sloan Review, "About the Culture 500," *Sloan Review*, https://sloanreview.mit.edu/culture500/research.
- Flurry, "Mobile Addicts Multiply Across the Globe," Flurry, July 15, 2015, https://www.flurry.com/blog/mobile-addicts-multiply-across -the-globe/.
- Alex Rolfe, "Bank of America—Trends in Consumer Mobility Report," Payments, Cards & Mobile, June 16, 2017, https://www.paymentscardsandmobile.com/bank-america-consumer-mobility -report/.
- Vera Gruessner, "71% of Consumers Sleep with Mobile Devices by the Bedside," mHealth Intelligence, August 27, 2015, https://mhealthintelligence.com/news/71-of-consumers-sleep-with-mobile -devices-by-the-bedside.
- Alan F., "Average Person Looks at His Phone 150 Times per Day," phoneArena.com, February 6, 2012, https://www.phonearena .com/news/Average-person-looks-at-his-phone-150-times-per-day _id26636.

- Ariel, "Why Storytelling Works: The Science," Ariel, https://www
.arielgroup.com/why-storytelling-works-the-science/.
- Vanessa Boris, "What Makes Storytelling So Effective for Learning?"
Harvard Business Publishing, December 20, 2017, https://www
.harvardbusiness.org/what-makes-storytelling-so-effective-for
-learning/.
- Paul J. Zak, "Why Your Brain Loves Good Storytelling," *Harvard
Business Review*, October 28, 2014, https://hbr.org/2014/10/why-your
-brain-loves-good-storytelling.
- Harrison Monarth, "The Irresistible Power of Storytelling as a
Strategic Business Tool," *Harvard Business Review*, March 11, 2014,
https://hbr.org/2014/03/the-irresistible-power-of-storytelling-as
-a-strategic-business-tool.
- Kristen Bahler, "Inside Amazon's Very Weird (but Very Efficient)
Staff Meetings," Money.com, February 5, 2020, https://money.com
/amazon-meetings-no-powerpoint/.
- Substack, "Creating a Writing Culture," Substack, August 16, 2019,
https://learnings.substack.com/p/creating-a-writing-culture.
- Business Insider, "Presenting: Satya Nadella Employed a 'Growth
Mindset' to Overhaul Microsoft's Cutthroat Culture and Turn It into
a Trillion-Dollar Company—Here's How He Did It," *Business Insider*,
March 8, 2020, https://www.businessinsider.com.au/microsoft-ceo
-satya-nadella-company-culture-shift-growth-mindset-2020-3.
- Ben Bashaw, "How Jeff Bezos Turned Narrative into Amazon's
Competitive Advantage," *Slab Blog*, February 5, 2019, https://slab
.com/blog/jeff-bezos-writing-management-strategy/.
- Tom Popomaronis, "Elon Musk Asks This Question at Every
Interview to Spot a Liar—Why Science Says It Actually Works,"
CNBC, January 26, 2021, https://www.cnbc.com/2021/01/26/elon
-musk-favorite-job-interview-question-to-ask-to-spot-a-liar-science
-says-it-actually-works.html.
- Satya Nadella, *Hit Refresh: The Quest to Rediscover Microsoft's
Soul and Imagine a Better Future for Everyone* (New York: Harper
Business, 2019).
- Ron Miller, "After 5 Years, Microsoft CEO Satya Nadella Has
Transformed More Than the Stock Price," Techcrunch, February 4,
2019, https://techcrunch.com/2019/02/04/after-5-years-microsoft
-ceo-satya-nadella-has-transformed-more-than-the-stock-price/.

- Jessica Schrader, "New Study Suggests Smiling Influences How You See the World," *Psychology Today*, August 14, 2020, https://www .psychologytoday.com/us/blog/the-right-mindset/202008/new-study -suggests-smiling-influences-how-you-see-the-world.
- Susan Sorenson, "How Employee Engagement Drives Growth," Gallup, June 20, 2013, https://www.gallup.com/workplace/236927 /employee-engagement-drives-growth.aspx.
- Harry Mccracken, "Satya Nadella Rewrites Microsoft's Code," Fast Company, September 8, 2017, https://www.fastcompany.com /40457458/satya-nadella-rewrites-microsofts-code.
- Justin Bariso, "Google Spent Years Studying Effective Teams. This Single Quality Contributed Most to Their Success," Inc., https://www .inc.com/justin-bariso/google-spent-years-studying-effective-teams -this-single-quality-contributed-most-to-their-success.html.
- Michael Schneider, "Google Spent 2 Years Studying 180 Teams. The Most Successful Ones Shared These 5 Traits," *Inc.*, https://www.inc .com/michael-schneider/google-thought-they-knew-how-to-create -the-perfect.html.
- Charles Duhigg, "What Google Learned from Its Quest to Build the Perfect Team," *New York Times Magazine*, February 25, 2016, https://www.nytimes.com/2016/02/28/magazine/what-google -learned-from-its-quest-to-build-the-perfect-team.html?.?mc= aud_dev&ad-keywords=auddevgate&gclid=Cj0KCQjw7MGJBhD -ARIsAMZ0eevF1mhPVTr46Ns13JL5o3sVw_8aLD0bZt2BbG _IbaanrkEz3hnOez0aAuMeEALw_wcB&gclsrc=aw.ds.

Chapter 8: Prepare to Go Exponential

- Rodney Scott, Lolis Eric Elie, and Rodney Scott, *World of BBQ* (Clarkson Potter; Illustrated edition, 2021).
- Rodney Scott, Lolis Eric Elie, and David Chang, *The David Chang Show* (Major Domo Media, 2021).
- David B. Wolfe, Jagdish Sheth, and Rajendra Sisodia, *Firms of Endearment: How World-Class Companies Profit from Passion and Purpose* (Pearson, 2014).
- Pete Thamel, "Wall Street to the Power Five? How Former CEO Joe Moglia Emerged as Coastal Carolina's Innovative Coach," *Sports Illustrated*, November 19, 2015, https://www.si.com/college/2015/11 /19/joe-moglia-could-coastal-carolina-coach-and-ex-ceo-be-primed -move-power-five.

- "Stone Tools," Human Origins, October 27, 2020, https://humanorigins.si.edu/evidence/behavior/stone-tools.
- "Industrial Revolution," Lumen Learning, https://courses.lumenlearning.com/boundless-ushistory/chapter/the-industrial-revolution/.
- Joel Mokyr, "The Second Industrial Revolution," WCAS, August 1998, https://faculty.wcas.northwestern.edu/~jmokyr/castronovo.pdf.
- Eric Niiler, "How the Second Industrial Revolution Changed Americans' Lives," History, January 25, 2019, https://www.history.com/news/second-industrial-revolution-advances.
- Stephane Garelli, "Why You Will Probably Live Longer Than Most Big Companies," IMD, December 2016, https://www.imd.org/research-knowledge/articles/why-you-will-probably-live-longer-than-most-big-companies/.

INDEX

ABOUT THE AUTHOR

JEFF ROSENBLUM is a founding partner of Questus, an agency that builds advertising for the modern consumer journey. Throughout his career, he has worked on strategic assignments for many of the world's most influential brands, including American Express, Apple, Capital One, Disney, ESPN, Ford, Gap, General Mills, Intel, Levi Strauss, Microsoft, the *New York Times*, the NFL, Salesforce, Samsung, *Sports Illustrated*, Starbucks, Suzuki, Universal, Verizon, the *Wall Street Journal*, and Wyndham.

Jeff created a documentary about the advertising revolution called *The Naked Brand* and wrote the book *Friction* (powerHouse Books, 2017), which explained how passion brands are built in the age of disruption.

Despite barely graduating college, Jeff has lectured at some of the top universities in the world, including Yale, Cornell, Columbia, and London Business School. His appearances at industry conferences have included Ad Age, ad:tech, TEDx, Inbound, and Digiday. His media appearances include Bloomberg TV, *Newsweek*, Fast Company, Glossy, Blaze TV, Cheddar, Ivy, EntreLeadership, and more.

Before starting Questus, Jeff went to the University of Vermont with his best friend and agency cofounder Jordan Berg. While there, he entered the Vermont Toughman Competition and got knocked out by someone much tougher than him. Apparently, it was worth it, because he gets to put it in this bio. In his free time, Jeff is addicted to learning new skills, including telemark skiing, screenwriting, fly fishing, and playing funk bass. His bass instructor succinctly summarizes the endeavors, describing his playing as "mediocre, at best."

Jeff serves on an advisory board for the Special Spectators, which provides sports experiences for kids facing life-threatening illnesses. He lives in New England with his wife, two kids, and dog, who are all much cooler and better looking than he is.